M366 Block 2
UNDERGRADUATE COMPUTING

Natural and artificial intelligence

Symbolic intelligence

Block

2

Cover image: Daniel H. Janzen. *Polistes* wasps build a relatively simple nest that lasts only a single summer. These New World wasps often site the unenclosed combs under eaves and the other sheltered places where they come into contact with people.

This publication forms part of an Open University course M366 *Natural and artificial intelligence*. Details of this and other Open University courses can be obtained from the Student Registration and Enquiry Service, The Open University, PO Box 197, Milton Keynes MK7 6BJ, United Kingdom: tel. +44 (0)845 300 6090, email general-enquiries@open.ac.uk

Alternatively, you may visit the Open University website at http://www.open.ac.uk where you can learn more about the wide range of courses and packs offered at all levels by The Open University.

To purchase a selection of Open University course materials visit http://www.ouw.co.uk, or contact Open University Worldwide, Michael Young Building, Walton Hall, Milton Keynes MK7 6AA, United Kingdom for a brochure. tel. +44 (0)1908 858793; fax +44 (0)1908 858787; email ouw-customer-services@open.ac.uk

The Open University
Walton Hall, Milton Keynes
MK7 6AA

First published 2007, second edition 2008.

Edited, designed and typeset by The Open University.

Printed and bound in the United Kingdom by The Charlesworth Group, Wakefield.

ISBN 978 0 7492 5068 3

2.1

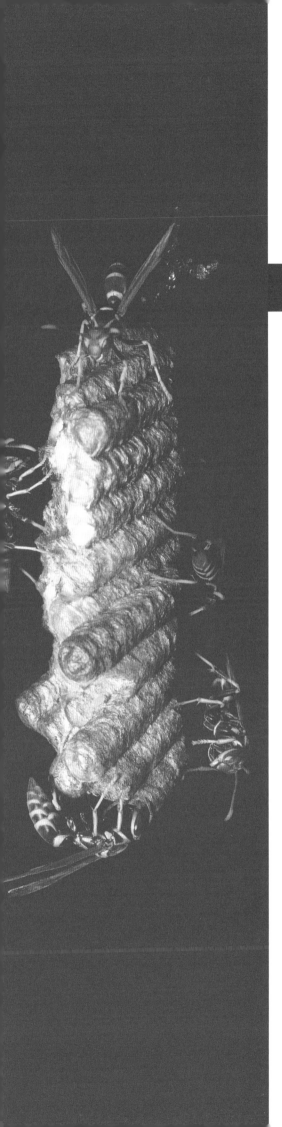

Block 2
Symbolic intelligence

Prepared for the course team by Neil Smith

CONTENTS

M366 COURSE TEAM

Chair, author and academic editor
Chris Dobbyn

Authors
Mustafa Ali

Tony Hirst

Mike Richards

Neil Smith

Patrick Wong

External assessor
Nigel Crook, Oxford Brookes University

Course managers
Gaynor Arrowsmith

Linda Landsberg

Media development staff
Andrew Seddon, Media Project Manager

Garry Hammond, Editor

Kate Gentles, Freelance Editor

Callum Lester, Software Developer

Andrew Whitehead, Designer and Graphic Artist

Phillip Howe, Compositor

Sarah Gamman, Contracts Executive

Lydia Eaton, Media Assistant

Critical readers
Frances Chetwynd

John Dyke

Ian Kenny

Paolo Remagnino

Thanks are due to the Desktop Publishing Unit of the Faculty of Mathematics and Computing.

Introduction to Block 2

Block introduction

This block is intended to give you an outline of the principles of, and progress in, Symbolic artificial intelligence (AI), as I defined it in Block 1. It is not my aim to go for comprehensive coverage of the subject – that would mean a course in itself. Rather, I want you to emerge from studying this block with a clear understanding of how the two conceptual pillars of Symbolic AI, representation and search, have been made to work in practice, and some of the successes, failures and drawbacks of the whole approach. This should provide a firm basis for the ideas in the rest of the course.

Unit 1: Fundamentals of Symbolic AI

The starting point of Symbolic AI is that problems can be explicitly represented in expressions that both people and machines can reason about. This approach has led to one particular mode of thinking about intelligence and problem solving: the physical symbol system hypothesis (PSSH). This strategy of explicit representation and reasoning is discussed in Unit 1, where the PSSH is introduced. In this unit I outline various systems of *representation*, mostly within the context of intelligent route-finding and game-playing systems.

Unit 2: Search

The concept of *search* is of key importance in Symbolic AI, as many problems in AI can be visualised as a search through a space of possible solutions to find the best one. Unit 2 discusses search and describes and analyses a number of specific search strategies.

Unit 3: Symbolic AI in the world

Unit 3 illustrates some successful computer systems based on Symbolic AI, including, among others, systems for planning, robotics and expert decision making.

Unit 4: Has Symbolic AI failed?

The block concludes by asking whether the project of Symbolic AI has failed. This leads to a discussion of the possible limitations of the Symbolic AI approach and sets the scene for the discussion of non-symbolic or 'nouvelle' AI that is the subject of the remainder of the course.

Block 2 learning outcomes

After studying this block you will be able to:

▶ write a paragraph describing the physical symbol system hypothesis and show how it relates to Symbolic AI;

▶ explain the separate roles of representation and reasoning in Symbolic AI;

▶ explain how search is a powerful reasoning system for Symbolic AI;

▶ draw diagrams illustrating some search algorithms and briefly outline their comparative strengths and weaknesses;

▶ describe, with diagrams, a number of applications of Symbolic AI;

▶ write a short essay laying out and reflecting on the perceived and actual shortcomings of Symbolic AI.

Unit 1: Fundamentals of Symbolic AI

CONTENTS

Introduction to Unit 1

In Block 1 I established that the goal of AI is 'to build intelligent machines'. I also gave some thought there to the question of what the word 'intelligence' could mean in this context, and how I might recognise intelligence in a machine. As you saw, the pioneers of the field I termed *Symbolic AI*, or just *AI* – Turing, von Neumann, Shannon, McCarthy and others – had few doubts as to the answers to these questions. They believed they had found a set of concepts that would enable them to realise the grand project of replicating intelligence on a machine. This block briefly tells the story of those concepts and that project.

This first unit of Block 2 is concerned with two of the key ideas that underpin Symbolic AI: **symbolic representation** and **symbolic reasoning**. I start by revisiting briefly the definition of 'intelligence' you were introduced to in Block 1, with a view to exploring its implications for AI. With the aid of two simple examples I then introduce the **physical symbol system hypothesis** (PSSH), the core principle of Symbolic AI.

As you learned in Block 1, one of the key ideas of Symbolic AI is the notion of *representation* – an idea that you will learn flows naturally from the PSSH. I move on to look in detail at this concept, considering the distinction between representation (expressing problems in sets of symbols) and reasoning (manipulating those symbols to find solutions to those problems). I then discuss how to design representations and then evaluate them. To close the discussion, I introduce the idea of representing the *knowledge* that humans bring to the solution of difficult and complex problems.

In the last section of the unit, I establish some of the basic ideas of *reasoning* with representations. As I suggested in Block 1, for many problems finding a good solution involves a *search* through a space of possible solutions. This approach, known as **heuristic search**, is introduced, to be discussed in much more detail in Unit 2.

What you need to study this unit

You will need the following course components, and will need to use your computer and internet connection for some of the exercises.

▶ this Block 2 text

▶ the course DVD.

LEARNING OUTCOMES FOR UNIT 1

After studying this unit you will be able to:

1.1 write a few sentences describing the physical symbol system hypothesis, showing how it relates to the project of Symbolic AI;

1.2 express certain selected problems as symbol manipulation tasks;

1.3 explain the separate roles of representation and reasoning in Symbolic AI;

1.4 write a paragraph explaining how knowledge is represented in intelligent systems, distinguishing between base-level knowledge and meta-knowledge;

1.5 critically discuss the comparative advantages and disadvantages of some example representations and reasoning methods.

2   What is intelligence?

In Block 1, I looked at some definitions of 'intelligence' and what it might mean for a human (or a machine) to be called intelligent. You saw straightaway that attempts at a catch-all definition quickly run into the sand, plagued by problems of disagreement, abstractness and circularity. Early AI scientists perhaps gave less thought to this problem than they might have done, but arrived fairly soon at a consensus about the answers to two basic questions:

▶ What is intelligence?

▶ How can we recognise intelligence in a machine?

To set the scene for this unit, consider this revision question.

SAQ 1.1

In a few sentences, summarise the answers the early AI scientists gave to these two questions.

ANSWER...

For Turing, McCarthy and others, intelligence was a matter of *behaviour*, of performing *activities* that could be called intelligent. They singled out two particular activities quite early on for special study: the ability to use language flexibly and the ability to play games, particularly chess, to a high level. The Turing Test was designed to probe the first of these capacities and became a gold standard for the recognition of intelligence.

One point emerged quite strongly from our discussions in Block 1. For Symbolic AI, the idea of intelligence has always been a matter of *human* intelligence, the ability of human beings to solve difficult problems of language, planning, organisation and design, often in situations of great complexity. Until quite recently, AI has tended to see the complex behaviour of animals and machines as being outside its sphere.

Exercise 1.1

Try to think of three kinds of problem that seem to need human intelligence to solve. Then try to think of three that you think do not require intelligence. Reflect on the reasons for your choice.

Discussion ....

Given the difficulty of pinning down the idea of intelligence, the number of possibilities is immense. Examples of complex problems that require intelligence might include winning at chess, currency trading, writing Open University course texts, getting high marks on TMAs for M366, organising a family to go on holiday, having a conversation about one of Shakespeare's sonnets, translating a text from English into French, finding a new oil field, diagnosing why your car won't start in the morning (and knowing what to do about it), selecting the best treatment for an injured patient, and many other such problems.

Thinking of tasks that we might not regard as requiring intelligence is even more challenging. Are such activities as digging a hole, riding a bike and finding baked beans in a supermarket fundamentally unintelligent? You might like to take the discussion to your tutor group or conference. Do other students agree with your choices?

As I'm sure you can see, there are all sorts of problems here. To go any deeper into them would take us too far away from our task in this block. But in summary, I thought the difficulties could be summed up by three questions:

▶ Are intelligent actions only ones that are *learnt* or could an *instinctive* (or semi-instinctive) behaviour such as walking be considered intelligent? We are inclined to think that solving an unfamiliar task needs intelligence of some kind, but as soon as we learn the technique to do it, it becomes routine and we no longer regard this as so.

▶ Are intelligent tasks only the ones that can only be done competently by a subset of 'intelligent' people, or do tasks that almost anyone can manage, such as speaking, planning or manipulating objects, require intelligence too? We'd all agree that Professor Stephen Hawking is pretty intelligent, the average *Big Brother* contestant maybe less so. But would we really want to rule out from the category of 'intelligence' everything except the kind of activities typical of Hawking's intellect?

▶ Is intelligence in some way related to *expertise*? We all admire the capacities of experts in their fields – doctors, scientists, musicians, and so on. Is it their *intelligence* we are admiring?

It would be out of place to discuss these questions any further here. As you'll discover, AI has traditionally tended to focus on a number of behaviours that have come to be labelled as, or are assumed to be, 'intelligent'. These include:

▶ **natural language processing**: the creation of machines capable of understanding and responding to human languages such as English;

▶ **expert problem solving**: for instance, diagnosing medical conditions from complex sets of symptoms;

▶ **planning** and scheduling tasks such as airline scheduling or planning the layout of a factory floor;

▶ **logical reasoning**, often under conditions of uncertainty.

In Block 3, I'll call into question some of the ideas I've just discussed. But with this tentative notion of 'intelligence' as a distinctively human set of behaviours for complex problem solving, we can now move into Block 2.

One of the main themes of this block, and this unit, is that intelligence comes from *knowledge* and the use of knowledge. Unfortunately, the definition of knowledge is every bit as slippery as the definition of intelligence: the term is used in countless different senses, in different contexts, by different people. In this unit, I will defer a discussion of knowledge until Section 8.1. By that time, you will have seen several examples of the ways that 'knowledge' can be incorporated into AI systems, and we should be able to use these examples to draw out possible interpretations of the term. Until then, you should keep your mind open on the role of knowledge in Symbolic AI.

This has been termed 'The AI problem' and the implications of this attitude are something we will return to in Unit 4 of this block.

Exercise 1.2

As you read this unit, note all the references to knowledge and its use. Think about the different ways it is used in different places. When you get to Section 8.1, compare your notes with the discussion in that section. Are they the same or different? Why? Are the differences important?

3 Examples of intelligent behaviour

In the last section, I settled on a working definition of 'intelligence' as a distinctively human set of behaviours for complex problem solving. But what sort of problems? As you will see, many of the problems we solve in everyday life are immensely complicated, and the range of them is vast. The ideal of creating an intelligent machine anywhere near as proficient as a typical human adult (one capable of passing the Turing test) is way beyond our reach at the moment. So instead, we have to set our sights lower and attempt something less ambitious, to identify certain quite limited problems that nevertheless seem to require intelligence to solve. You may remember that this was one of McCarthy's strategic proposals in the original Dartmouth prospectus. Concentrating on building systems that can tackle quite small-scale, although still difficult problems may allow us to draw out some of the key features of human intelligence and start us on the road to emulating such intelligence in machines.

The Turing Test was discussed in Section 4.1 in Block 1.

3.1 Interior design

The task of arranging furniture in a room is surely one that requires some intelligence, especially if we want the final arrangement to fulfil particular criteria, such as using space efficiently, being able to reach all the drawers in cabinets easily, and so on. An obvious approach is to physically move the furniture around the room until we get an arrangement that satisfies us. The obvious drawback of this is that this is a lot of hard work, especially if we need to try out many different arrangements before deciding on what works best. Much of this effort can be saved by developing *symbols* to represent the pieces of furniture; manipulating symbols of furniture should be much easier than manipulating the furniture itself, so we can save our backs!

One symbol-based approach, then, would be to create scale models of the room and the items in it. We can rearrange these until a pleasing design is achieved. When we are satisfied with the arrangement, we can move the real pieces of furniture into the new positions indicated by the final state of our model. In this approach, the models are the symbols and the scaled space we are working in has exactly the same constraints as the real space: we can no more put two model chairs in the same place than two real chairs.

A more economical way of representing the room would be to draw a scale plan of it on a sheet of paper and to cut out little card shapes of all the pieces of furniture (similar to Figure 1.1). Each shape is then a symbol representing a single piece of furniture and the plan is a symbol that represents the room.

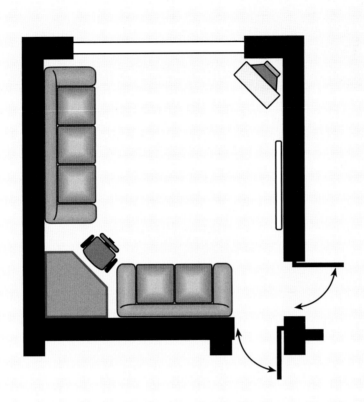

Figure 1.1 Plan of a room and its contents

Such a representation is easier to create, but it requires a little more mental work to imagine what the final arrangement will look like. It also forces us to enforce some constraints on the way the furniture symbols can be arranged. For example, no cut-out should overlap the boundary of the room plan, and no two pieces should overlie each other: pieces of card may overlap each other easily, but armchairs are unlikely to act in the same way. We might also want to ensure that all the pieces remain flat on the paper: we may turn over an L-shaped piece of card to fit it better into a gap, but inverting the sofa it corresponds to will be neither easy nor useful. This constraint might be useful if we also want to see how the furniture should be moved from the old layout into the new one.

We may adopt approximate versions of this system of representation, for example by quickly sketching the desired layout on the back of an envelope. This has the advantage of speed, but it may not be accurate enough. Finally, the most abstract kind of symbolic representation might be to encode the dimensions of the room and the furniture into a computer-aided design (CAD) package and do the arrangement of furniture entirely in a virtual world.

There is one further hitch. How do we know when to stop trying out different solutions? At one extreme, we may find that more or less *any* way of arranging the furniture in the room satisfies the constraints on the problem. At the other, we might have to examine every possible arrangement of all the furniture in the room in order to be sure that we have found the best one (by some as-yet-undetermined definition of 'best'). In practice, we could try a few possible solutions, modifying good ones, until we got one that seems good enough. As you learned in Block 1, we often have to settle for solutions that are merely 'good' rather than being the best.

3.2 | Route planning

Finding the best route from A to B is another problem that seems to require intelligence to solve. Planning a route from Exeter to Inverness, say, is clearly not an easy task when there are so many alternative routes that seem plausible. Determining which is the best route can be the source of interminable debate among men of a certain age in the pub: 'Go straight down the main road ...' 'No, it's shorter if you go around behind the supermarket and pick up the bypass ...'

This 'send many agents' approach will be considered in Block 3.

As for the furniture-arranging problem, the most direct way to solve this problem is to try all the routes, either by having one person try them one after the other, or by sending many people simultaneously, each on a different route. In reality, most strategies involve working with some form of symbolic representation. Maps (e.g. Figure 1.2) are the most commonly used symbolic representation of routes.

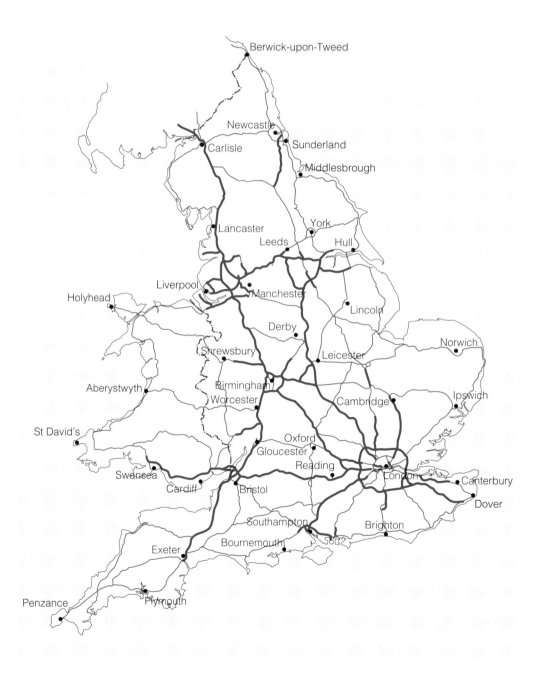

Figure 1.2   A road map of England and Wales

Given a map that shows the starting point, the destination and all the routes between them, we can start to see which routes are long or short and so predict which will be the shortest. But a map is not the territory itself: it is only a *model* of the ground it represents and every map is necessarily inaccurate to some degree. This means that after we've taken the decision to use a map, there are still decisions to be made about what sort of map, what scale it should have and whether it should include information on types of road or heights. The larger the scale, the greater the detail that can be captured on the map and the more accurate will be our estimates of distance. Conversely, smaller-scale maps will show less detail and will lead to less accurate estimates, but the map itself will be smaller and so easier to manipulate and view. Once we have the map, we can measure the distances between points with something like a piece of string, and from these calculate the shortest route.

But a map is not necessarily the easiest representation to use for this problem. If all we are really interested in is the *length* of the shortest route from A to B (or from A to C then from C to B), we can simply look up those distances on a route-planner table, rather like the one for the Travelling Salesman Problem that you met in Block 1, and repeated here as Table 1.1.

Of Exactitude in Science is an extremely short (one paragraph) story by Jorge Luis Borges and Adolfo Bioy Cesares of a map that was in 1:1 scale with the empire it represented. Naturally, it was useless.

Table 1.1 Distances table for the shortest route problem

	Exeter	Bristol	Manchester	Leeds	London
Exeter	X	74	236	278	173
Bristol	74	X	165	207	119
Manchester	236	165	X	43	198
Leeds	278	207	43	X	195
London	173	119	198	195	X

Similarly to our interior design problem, here we have a set of quite different representations. One key difference between the map and the table will be in the *operations* they allow or encourage.

SAQ 1.2

What factors do you need to consider when using a symbolic representation for route planning? What factors should you consider when *creating* these symbolic representations?

ANSWER..

When using the map-based representation, we need to consider which features on the map are relevant to our decision making. Should we concern ourselves with whether a given road goes up a hill? Do we plan our route with preferences for different types of road?

When creating the map, we need to decide what scale to use, whether to include minor routes (bridleways, single-track roads or anything other than a trunk road), and so on.

When creating the table of distances, the first thing to consider is which destinations to include. We also have to select the route that will be taken between each pair of destinations. As with the map, we have to decide which routes will be available. Should we, for instance, prefer a slightly longer route on a motorway to a shorter one on a B-road?

The general idea of 'going from A to B' is a powerful one, as A and B need not be physical locations. Finding a route from 'empty car and a pile of suitcases' to 'packed car' is useful, if the 'route' is described in terms of what objects to pack when. Finding a 'route', a sequence of moves, from the starting position in chess to a winning position results in winning the game. Route finding is an analogy that is often used in Symbolic AI and it is a theme that I will return to again and again in this block.

4 The physical symbol system hypothesis

In Block 1, I noted that perhaps the most effective way of defining intelligence is in terms of examples of intelligent behaviour. Rather than finding some form of words that completely encapsulates our idea of intelligence, instead we offer up instances of various kinds of intelligent *actions* people can perform. Descartes and Turing thought that the human capacity to converse naturally and flexibly through language was at the core of human intelligence; for Shannon and others the ability to play chess well was a clear indication of intelligence at work. And, as I noted in the introduction to this unit, there are many other kinds of intelligent behaviour that AI scientists have tried to replicate on machines, including:

▶ natural language processing

▶ expert problem solving

▶ logical reasoning

▶ planning and scheduling.

This list is by no means exhaustive. One might add, for example:

▶ visual processing and recognition

▶ controlling physical movement.

You can see that I'm construing the idea of 'behaviour' quite broadly. You might be inclined to think that the word refers only to *physical* actions – doing something with one's body, possibly mindlessly – like a lab rat finding cheese in a maze or a hamster running on a wheel. But although these are indeed forms of behaviour, so too are activities we associate with mental life, such as speaking, playing chess, sitting quietly trying to work out the answer to a Sudoku puzzle, or even recognising a friend's face.

Although the kinds of behaviour suggested above seem pretty disparate, we would probably all agree that they require intelligence of some kind. But how does this work? What role is intelligence playing? Well, one conventional view of intelligence is that it is a process of:

1   taking in information from the world;

2   processing it some sophisticated way and identifying a sensible solution;

3   doing something with the solution.

But the intelligence all seems to lie in Step 2. It's surely all to do with that processing phase, where the solution is discovered. Intelligence is a mental thing – all in the head. Whether it is *consciously* in the head is another matter, though. When I try to solve a crossword puzzle, or play chess, I'm fully aware of what I'm doing, of the logical steps that I'm taking as I ponder what to do next. But when I'm in a conversation, or examining a diagram, exactly what mental processes are going on are much less clear to me – I'm just talking; I'm just seeing. However, this need not affect the issue. The fact that I may not be aware of the processes that are going on between my ears does not necessarily mean they aren't happening.

Our three-step procedure above looks so much like the familiar 'input–process–output' model of computation that the idea that intelligence can be embedded in a computer-based system seems promising. Advances in logic and theoretical computer science in the first half of the twentieth century offered a formal basis for this intuition. These advances, and the key hypothesis of Symbolic AI, were clearly articulated by Alan Newell and Herb Simon, in a classic address to the ACM in 1975, where they put forward and defended what has come to be known as the **physical symbol system hypothesis (PSSH)**.

ACTIVITY 1.1

You will find instructions for locating the paper 'Computer science as empirical inquiry: symbols and search' (Newell and Simon, 1976) on the course DVD. Look through this paper. You may wish to read the whole paper, but Section 1, 'Symbols and physical symbol systems', is what we will be concentrating on. If you don't want to read all of Section 1, you need only read the subsections 'Physical symbol systems' and 'The evidence' to follow the discussion below. However, I will also refer to the ideas from the subsections 'Laws of qualitative structure' and 'Development of the symbol systems hypothesis'.

As you read, jot down notes about the meanings of the following terms, as Newell and Simon use them here:

▶ symbol
▶ symbol structure
▶ expression
▶ object
▶ designation
▶ process
▶ interpretation
▶ the physical symbol system hypothesis.

Figure 1.3   Alan Newell (right) and Herb Simon discussing computer chess in 1958

Recall that in Block 1 I've defined a 'model' as 'a simplified picture of some aspect of reality'.

Newell and Simon begin by noting that the aim of all science is to pin down the essential facts of some aspect of nature. These facts, they claim, can generally be captured in a short and simple statement. To use an idea that is already familiar to you from Block 1, the aim of scientific enquiry is, first and foremost, to build a *model* of the phenomena being studied. In just the same way as a computer model is a pared-down representation of some real-world problem, scientific models are simplified descriptions of structures and events in the world. A good model captures everything that is important about the phenomena in question, while leaving out everything that is irrelevant and that would stand in the way of understanding.

Newell and Simon propose just such a model of an intelligent system, which they call a **symbolic system** or a **physical symbol system**. Taking their definition one step at a time:

1   They start with the concept of a **symbol**, defining this simply as some entity that exists in the real world and obeys the laws of physics. So a symbol could be a word, a signpost of some kind, an electrochemical event in the brain, a charge state of a transistor or capacitor, a tin can – more or less anything we want.

2   Symbols can be gathered together into **symbol structures** or **expressions** – the two terms seem to be interchangeable. It's best just to see an expression as an ordered and structured collection of symbols. A collection of expressions adds up to a **physical symbol system**.

3   Expressions (which can be single symbols) **designate** things in the world, which Simon and Newell term **objects**. Simon and Newell's actual definition of 'designation' is rather involved; but I think it really amounts to no more than the idea that symbol expressions *stand for* or *represent* other things. For example, the symbol expression 'Schrödinger' designates a certain grey cat living in Milton Keynes in 2006, while the symbol in Figure 1.4 actually represents quite a complex idea (rather than a physical object).

4   Not all expressions designate objects. Some expressions specify **processes** that operate on other expressions within the physical symbol system.

5   When a process operates on an expression, it can modify it, produce a completely new expression or delete the expression altogether. The task of identifying a process, applying it to an expression and so changing the expression in some way is termed **interpretation**.

6   Since processes can manipulate any symbol structure, including those that represent processes, then physical symbol systems are capable of manipulating not only the designations of objects, but also their own processes. In other words, physical symbol systems are capable of self-interpretation.

You may remember this notion came up briefly in the discussion of Thomas Hobbes' ideas in Block 1.

Figure 1.4 A commonly seen symbol representing 'the national speed limit'

Note how this idea of interpretation implies the notion of the system progressing in discrete stages. When a process is interpreted, the system discretely changes to the new state. I will return to the idea of states and transitions between them later, particularly in Unit 2.

SAQ 1.3

Briefly explain what is meant by a *symbol* and then spend the next few minutes thinking about what the main characteristics of symbols might be.

ANSWER..

In Block 1, I defined a symbol as 'something that stands for something else'. For example, the symbol '5' stands for the number five, the symbol '£' stands for pounds (sterling), and the symbol '©' stands for copyright. By 'standing for', I mean 'indicating' or 'representing'.

The three main characteristics of a symbol are *atomicity*, *arbitrariness* and *persistence*: a symbol is atomic or indivisible because it cannot be further divided into other symbols and because it is discrete, which means that it can be separated and distinguished from other symbols; symbols are arbitrary because they are established by agreement or convention based on selection from among alternatives; a symbol is persistent because it continues to exist until such time as it is destroyed, either deliberately or through lack of use.

Another definition of a symbol is 'an arbitrary (or conventional) sign', where *sign* is taken to mean 'something that stands for something else for some agent (such as a human, animal, computer or robot) for some purpose'. I will look again at this definition in Block 6 in connection with the symbol-grounding problem, which is the problem of how symbols get their meaning.

SAQ 1.4

Which of the following can be used as a symbol for the number three?

γ

3

٣

4

three

ANSWER..

All of the above are – or *can be* – used as symbols for the number three with the exception of the word 'three' which, strictly speaking, isn't a symbol since it is made up of four letters, 't', 'h', 'r' and 'e', each of which is itself a symbol. (Remember that in SAQ 1.3 we saw that one of the characteristics of a symbol is that it is atomic.) However, it makes a perfectly good symbol expression. γ is the Greek letter gamma, which stood for the number three in the Ancient Greek language; **3** is the symbol for the number three in the dominant system of numerals in use throughout the modern world; ٣ is the symbol for the number three in Arabic (whose system of numerals is Indian in origin); and **4** *can be* – although in most, if not all, contexts *should not be* – used to stand for the number three. (Remember that in SAQ 1.3 we saw that another important characteristic of symbols is that they are arbitrary, that is, established by convention.) In fact, anything that is atomic, arbitrary and persistent – in short, anything that is a symbol – *can* stand for the number three.

Summing up, then, a physical symbol system is a collection of symbols and symbol structures. Certain symbols or symbol structures designate objects in the real world; others represent processes that can occur. The combination of all the symbol expressions within a physical symbol system determines the system's **state**. The state evolves over time as processes within the system (also expressed as symbols and symbol structures) operate on it. The set of states that a physical symbol system can be in is termed the system's **state space**, with the system occupying one of those states at any particular time.

A pictorial summary of the relationship between the world and physical symbol systems is given in Figure 1.5.

Does this sound at all familiar? Think back to Block 1 and our description there of the computer as an *interpreted, automatic formal system*. You might care to glance back at this. I used a slightly different terminology there, but if I substitute the word 'symbol' for 'token', 'processes' for 'rules', and so on, it is clear that Simon and Newell's physical symbol system is a formal system, in the sense I described in Block 1. Moreover, since a physical symbol system is able to manipulate, and thus apply, its own processes, it is an automatic system; and since certain symbols and expressions designate objects in the world, a physical symbol system is an interpreted system too. A digital computer *is* a physical symbol system.

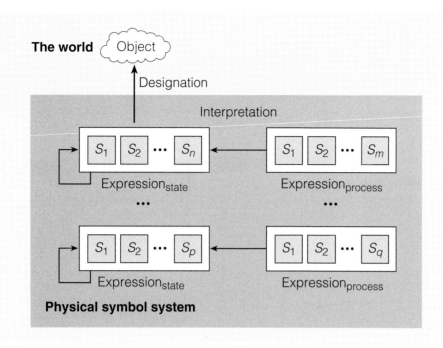

Figure 1.5   Relationship between physical symbol systems and the world. S_1, S_2, etc. denote symbols which are physical patterns and the feedback loops indicate a change of state

But Newell and Simon took this idea much further with their physical symbol system hypothesis (PSSH). They proposed that symbolic logic is a model of how humans use their intelligence when solving problems: humans form a symbolic mental representation of the problem, they claimed, and then manipulate that representation to discover solutions. In other words, humans *are* physical symbol manipulation systems. Even more daringly, they proposed that *any* (sufficiently large) physical symbol manipulation system can be intelligent, regardless of the physical 'hardware' it uses. They also suggested that *all* intelligent systems will, on close analysis, be found to be physical symbol systems. In Newell and Simon's own words, 'a physical symbol system has the necessary and sufficient means for general intelligent action.'

Exercise 1.3

Name three other physical symbol systems you know about.

Discussion ....

If you have had some difficulty coming up with examples, rest assured that you are not alone – members of the course team also struggled with this activity! One of the reasons why this appears to be such a difficult question is that the PSSH seems *anthropocentric* in that it conceives intelligence in human-centred terms. As you might have noticed, Newell and Simon only present two examples of physical symbol systems in their paper: human beings and a particular class of machines *made by* human beings – computers. Whether or not there are any other physical symbol systems depends on whether symbols (as physical patterns) and associated mechanisms for processing symbol-structures (or expressions) exist 'out there' in the world, independently of human beings. (I will investigate this issue in more detail in Block 6.) If one accepts that they do, then symbols and symbol-processing are clearly very widespread because physical symbol systems are no longer exclusively human or human-constructed phenomena; physical symbol systems now include *natural* phenomena. (I will briefly examine the distinction between natural and artificial phenomena in Block 3.)

From this point of view, an ant colony might be an example of a natural physical symbol system, where the symbols are *either* individual ants *or* groups of ants. However, as we shall see in Block 3, there are other ways to think about intelligence in natural systems (such as ant colonies) that do not require us to make use of the PSSH.

In other papers, Newell and Simon state explicitly that they think that human brains and computers are fundamentally equivalent:

> Our situation is one of defining a symbol system to be a universal machine, and then taking as a hypothesis that this notion of symbol system will prove adequate to all of the symbolic activity this physical universe of ours can exhibit, and in particular all the symbolic activities of the human mind.
>
> Source: Newell (1980, p. 155)

and:

> The computer is a member of an important family of artefacts called symbol systems, or more explicitly, *physical symbol systems*. Another important member of the family (some of us think, anthropomorphically, it is the *most* important) is the human mind and brain.
>
> Source: Simon (1981)

Newell goes on:

> That humans are physical symbol systems implies that there exists a physical architecture that supports that symbol system ... there must exist a neural organization that is an architecture – i.e. that supports a symbol structure.
>
> Source: Newell (1980, p. 174)

You should note, however, that the PSSH is only that – a hypothesis. It is a proposal for what Newell and Simon believe is a good candidate for the underpinnings of intelligence. In the remainder of their paper, Newell and Simon outline some of the implications of adopting the PSSH and how it should guide experiments in AI research.

Exercise 1.4

Spend the next few minutes thinking about the PSSH. Do you think that it is true? Briefly explain your answer.

Discussion ....

In my view, it's not so important for the PSSH to be true in some absolute sense as it is for it to be *useful*. In short, even if the hypothesis is false, it might still be of practical value in that it can be successfully applied to a range of problems. As Newell and Simon point out in the article you looked at in Activity 1.1, computer science – which includes the building of purportedly intelligent systems – is an *empirical*, that is, experimental and pragmatic, discipline. For me, the validity of the hypothesis is dependent on whether it delivers workable solutions to real problems. Given the successful application of this hypothesis in the design and construction of many AI systems, I think it is fair to say that the physical symbol system hypothesis has value.

For the purposes of this block, I will adopt the PSSH as my working model of how to build intelligent systems. I will explore its implications, in particular how it guides attempts to build intelligent machines, and the strengths and limitations of those machines. I consider some weaknesses of the hypothesis itself in the final unit.

Exercise 1.5

What type of problem do you think physical symbol systems can potentially solve? Hint: in order to answer this question, think about the implications of one of the main characteristics of symbols discussed in SAQ 1.3.

Discussion ....

Since physical symbol systems make use of symbols which are atomic or discrete in nature, only those problems that are capable of being expressed atomically – that is, discretely – can potentially be solved using a physical symbol system.

5 Representation and reasoning

The physical symbol system hypothesis PSSH is a powerful way of modelling how intelligent entities work. The notion of manipulating expressions (symbol structures) allows us to ignore the physical underpinnings of the intelligent system, such as the hardware it uses, or the programming language it is written in. Provided that the system is physically realisable, all that is important is the interrelations between the symbols and therefore the expressions that they form. This frees us from having to deal with matters that are irrelevant.

SAQ 1.5

Assuming the PSSH is correct, try to identify the symbols in the following physical systems:

▶ a mammalian brain

▶ a computer

▶ an ant colony.

What are the symbolic expressions in each of these systems?

ANSWER..

As you will recall from Section 4, the PSSH states that symbols are physical patterns, so for the physical systems given in the list, the symbols might be:

▶ patterns of nervous activity;

▶ charge states of transistors and capacitors;

▶ individual ants (or groups of ants).

However, remember that according to the PSSH, the *form* of symbols, which depends on what the physical system is made of, is irrelevant to the *role* that they play in the system – provided that the basic symbol-structures can be processed. All that matter are purely *structural* arrangements of symbols. Hence, for each of the physical systems in the above list, the symbolic expressions are precisely that – structures of symbols.

The other advantage that comes from adopting the PSSH is the separation of expressions into two kinds: expressions that depict objects and expressions that can be interpreted as processes. This allows us to separate the problem of building intelligent machines into two parts. We need to design:

▶ the expressions that represent the world;

▶ the processes that reason about those designating expressions.

However, this does not in any way restrict the form that the representation must take. The PSSH merely demands that the symbol expressions represent the entities we are interested in. Indeed, there will generally be *many* possible representations for a particular problem. Section 7 outlines a couple of examples and the different expressions we could use to represent them.

Once we have a representation of the problem domain and some processes we can perform, we can start to see how the problem-solving process can take place. For instance, consider the 'water jugs' problem described in Box 1.1. For this problem, we don't need to consider the shapes or colours of the jugs, or how much water is in the barrel.

Box 1.1: The 'water jugs' problem

You have a large barrel of water and two jugs. One jug holds exactly four litres when full to the brim, the other three litres. Neither jug is graduated, and you can't mark the jugs. You can fill jugs from the barrel. You can pour water from one jug to the other jug, onto the floor or back into the barrel.

You have to end up with two litres of water in one of the jugs. How do you do it?

Figure 1.6 The water jugs problem

In this problem, the objects of interest are the barrel, the two jugs, their capacities and the water level in each. The processes are filling jugs from the barrel, emptying jugs and pouring water from one jug to another (stopping when one jug is either full or empty). Everything else (the capacity of the barrel, for example) is an irrelevant detail.

We start with a set of expressions that describe the starting situation: the barrel is full and both jugs are empty. We can change this state of affairs by performing one of the processes: for instance, we could fill the four-litre jug from the barrel. By doing so, the process will move us to a new state: the four-litre jug is now full. There are several processes we could perform as the next step. We could pour three litres of water into the smaller jug, or fill the smaller jug from the barrel, or empty the large jug. Any of these will change the state again. And so we continue, step by step, with processes changing the state of affairs at each step, until we end up in a state (the *goal state*) where one jug contains two litres of water. The list of steps taken in transforming the initial state to the goal state then becomes the solution to the problem.

Exercise 1.6

Write down a sequence of steps that solves the water jugs problem.

Discussion ....

I had this sequence of steps:

1 Fill the four-litre jug.

2 Pour water from the four-litre jug into the three-litre jug until the smaller one is full. This leaves one litre in the four-litre jug.

3 Empty the three-litre jug.

4 Pour the remaining water (one litre) from the four-litre jug into the three-litre jug.

5 Refill the four-litre jug.

6 Pour water from the four-litre jug into the three-litre jug until it is full. You must have poured two litres into the smaller jug to fill it, which means that two litres must remain in the four-litre jug.

Note that, in adopting the physical symbol hypothesis as the basis of our thinking about problem solving, we have made a fundamental assumption about the *nature* of problems and their solutions. We have assumed that the state of a problem can be designated by a particular arrangement of symbol expressions, and that processes can be interpreted as transforming one designation into another. Thus problem solving progresses in discrete steps, which also means that we must design our reasoning systems in terms of taking discrete steps, which simplifies matters.

If we can describe the states that are possible, and we know how one state is transformed into another by a particular process, we can describe the **state space** of a problem as a **graph**: a set of **nodes** each representing a specific state and **arcs** connecting the nodes and representing processes that can be applied to that state to transform it into another. The state space is simply the set of all possible states and the possible transformations between them. Figure 1.7 shows the state space of the water jugs problem. It gives us a visual intuition of how to go about solving this sort of problem: we start in some initial state (node 00) and move along the lines through the problem's state space, looking for a goal state (nodes 24, 20, 02 or 32). I'll come back to this idea in Section 9, and one solution to this problem, *search*, is the focus of Unit 2.

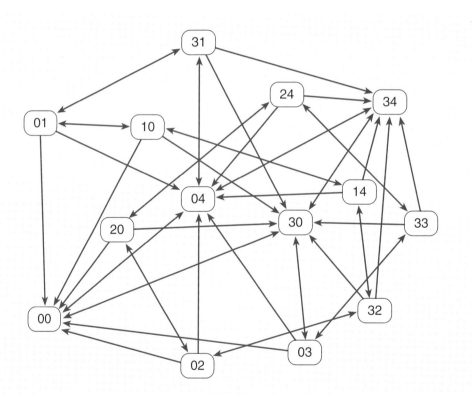

Figure 1.7 The state space of the water jugs problem. The numbers in each node are the amount of water in the three- and four-litre jugs, respectively

Now you've got the idea of how to represent problems, let's look at another classic one, the missionaries-and-cannibals problem (outlined in Box 1.2).

Box 1.2: Missionaries-and-cannibals problem

During a trip, three missionaries are guided by three locals. Unfortunately for the missionaries, the locals are cannibals and will eat the missionaries if they ever outnumber the latter. The party comes to a river crossing. The one boat available takes only two people, one of whom is required to row it from one side of the river to the other.

How can all six people cross the river without anyone being eaten?

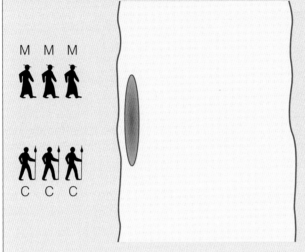

Figure 1.8   The initial state of the missionaries-and-cannibals problem

Exercise 1.7

Spend a few minutes thinking about how to represent the missionaries-and-cannibals problem. Identify all the important *objects* and *processes* in the problem. Which features are important? Which are irrelevant?

Discussion ....

The objects are the missionaries, the cannibals and the boat. The number of missionaries and cannibals on each side of the river is clearly important, as is which side of the river the boat is on. We don't need to include details of the river crossing itself, such as how long it takes. In fact, we only need to record who and what is on the starting side of the river, as we can work out who is on the other side. The only operation is moving the boat from one side to the other, with one or two people aboard.

The solution to this problem is given in Unit 2. However, you might want to have a go at solving it on your own. An online version is available at:

http://www.plastelina.net/games/game2.html

All this leaves us with several questions about representations. For example, how do we go about developing a representation, and what makes a good representation? It also leaves us with the deeper question of what reasoning processes will quickly find a series of steps to take us from the initial state to the goal state. I discuss representations in the next section; how to reason efficiently is covered in Section 9.

6 | Developing representations

There is another aspect we have to decide on, which is how to choose between the processes that are possible at any particular stage. This is something I will cover further when I discuss meta-reasoning in Section 9.

As I claimed above, representations (stated as symbolic expressions) can stand for two kinds of thing: *objects* in the domain of interest and *processes* that work on those objects. For any problem, then, once we have decided on what each of these are – when we are able to describe what we know and how to reason about it – then intelligent reasoning becomes possible.

Exercise 1.8

Consider an expert system (a computer system that captures some human expertise, discussed in Section 7.2) designed to diagnose faults in a car and offer suggestions on how to remedy them. Try to identify some of the objects that might be important in this domain and some of the processes that we might like our expert system to perform.

Discussion ....

The objects that might be important in this domain include facts about the car, questions that could be asked and the answers to those questions. The processes that we might like the expert system to perform include asking questions, performing inferences and suggesting tests or remedies.

The exercise shows that any representation we choose will be intimately connected to questions about what we want our system to *do*. Obviously, we want to find a representation that completely supports all the tasks we have in mind for the system, and moreover allows them to be performed efficiently. These sorts of design decisions are universal in computing, and – as I'm sure you appreciate – are more art than science. However, the sorts of problems addressed by AI systems, ones that require intelligence to perform, are often even harder to analyse than traditional programming problems. The solutions to AI problems tend to be more sophisticated and subtle than those of normal programming practice.

So, to develop a suitable representation for a problem, we have to determine the objects to be represented, the relationships between those objects, any important attributes of these objects and relationships, and the ways all these objects and relationships fit together to form a complete picture of the problem. One consideration is how much information should be *explicit* in the representation, and how much we could just *infer* from the explicit facts when required. For instance, in the water jugs example, we know three things about each jug: its capacity, how much water is in it and how much space remains. We could record these three facts for each jug, or we could rely on the fact that we can infer the third from the other two. It is a design decision as to which we do.

Exercise 1.9

Spend the next few minutes thinking about the advantage of information being kept implicit in a problem representation. What might be the disadvantage?

Discussion ....

The advantage is in updating the state, as there is less information to manipulate and keep consistent. The disadvantage is that the implicit information needs to be inferred if we need it, which costs computing time and resources.

Clearly we also have to develop representations of the *processes* that manipulate these states, so that we can transform the initial state into the goal state. And these processes must be specified in such a way that they preserve the constraints in the problem domain. For example, in the jugs problem, we have to ensure that the amount of water is conserved when pouring it from one jug to another.

Another design issue is that different representations may be appropriate to different tasks. Each choice of representation may highlight a particular aspect of the problem at the expense of others. Hopefully, a good choice will highlight those aspects that are important for solving the problem at hand. A good example of this is the mutilated chessboard problem. First, we consider the intact chessboard problem.

Exercise 1.10

Imagine you have a chessboard and thirty-two dominoes (see Figure 1.9). Each domino exactly covers two squares on the chessboard. Can you use the thirty-two dominoes to cover the chessboard, so that each square is covered and no dominoes overlap?

Figure 1.9   A standard chessboard

Discussion ....

If we use a representation of the board that conceptually divides it into rows and squares, it's quite easy to see that the answer is yes. One domino covers two squares, four dominoes placed end-to-end will cover one row of the chessboard, so the $4 \times 8 = 32$ dominoes will cover the entire board.

If we now mutilate the chessboard, by cutting off two diagonally opposite corner squares (see Figure 1.10), we have the mutilated chessboard problem: can you cover the chessboard with only 31 dominoes?

Exercise 1.11

Can you cover the mutilated chessboard with thirty-one dominoes? Spend a few minutes thinking of a solution.

Discussion ....

In fact, the mutilated chessboard problem is impossible: you cannot cover the mutilated board with thirty-one dominoes.

If you represent the chessboard in the same way as in Exercise 1.10 (a collection of rows, each made up of squares), you will find that you need to spend a long time checking all possible arrangements of dominoes in case one of them is successful. However, by changing the representation of the board, you can quickly arrive at a proof that the mutilated chessboard problem is impossible. This alternative solution considers the colour of the squares on the chessboard.

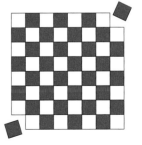

Figure 1.10   The mutilated chessboard

Exercise 1.12

Each domino covers two squares. Each of these squares could be black or white. Write down all the possible combinations of colours that a single domino can cover.

Discussion ....

This exercise shouldn't have taken you long. If every domino exactly covers two squares, every domino must cover one white and one black square.

This gives us a clue as to an alternative representation of the board that may be more useful for this particular problem: we count the number of black and white squares. Each domino covers two squares: one white and one black. A normal chessboard has thirty-two white squares and thirty-two black squares, so it might be possible to cover it with thirty-two dominoes. The mutilated chessboard has had two black squares removed, leaving it with thirty-two white squares and thirty black ones.

Exercise 1.13

Given this representation, prove that it is impossible to cover the mutilated chessboard with thirty-one dominos.

Discussion ....

We could lay thirty dominos, which would cover sixty of the squares: thirty white and thirty black. However, that would leave two white squares uncovered. As we know that every domino must cover one black and one white square, we know that it is impossible to lay the thirty-first domino to cover these remaining squares.

Another factor that has to be represented in many situations is uncertainty, whether it is uncertainty about what we know or uncertainty about the results of our actions. I'll briefly look at how this is handled in Section 5 of Unit 3.

The point of this example is to show that our choice of representation can have a great impact on the sort of reasoning a system can perform (and the computational cost of it). Some representations, such as a count of the numbers of squares of different colours, allowed us to easily determine that some problems are impossible. Other representations, such as the row-and-square model, were more informative about the way to actually lay out the dominos.

7 Examples of symbol representations

The preceding discussion was rather abstract. In order to make the ideas clearer, I will now examine some examples of symbolic representations. When you're reading about these problems, ask yourself what would constitute intelligent behaviour in solving them? Would finding any solution be sufficient, or is there a need to pick the best solution from many?

7.1 Playing chess

As you learned in Block 1, chess is *the* classic problem of AI. It has been studied since the very earliest days of AI research, partly at least because of its reputation as a game requiring high levels of intelligence to play well. But in Block 1 I also suggested that chess is an ideal problem for a computerised symbolic system to tackle. A digital computer is an interpreted automatic formal system. Chess, too, is a formal system: it is *discrete*, *medium-independent*, *self-contained* and *finitely playable*.

The senses in which I'm using these terms were explained in Block 1 and are in the Glossary.

So our task now is to find a form of representation that will provide all the information a computer system needs to play the game of chess. What would work well?

Exercise 1.14

Spend 5 to 10 minutes sketching a suitable form of symbolic representation for the game of chess. I'm not expecting you to go into any great detail, so you don't need to be any kind of chess expert, or really even to know the rules of the game. Think about the basics. It might help to refer to Figure 1.11, which shows a fairly typical chess position.

Figure 1.11   A chess position

Discussion ....

We have to find symbolic expressions that can stand for the state of the board at any one time, such as the position reached in Figure 1.11. Of course, there are lots of ways to do this: one fairly obvious one, for instance, would be set up a group of 64 statements, one for each square of the board (a1–h8), each expression describing what, if anything, is on that square. For this, we would just need to assign a symbol to stand for each kind

= King = K

= Queen = Q

= Bishop = B

= Rook = R

= Knight = N

= Pawn = P

Figure 1.12 Symbols representing pieces

of piece, as in the key shown in Figure 1.12 and the symbols 'w' and 'b' to stand for 'white' and 'black'. Then, for the position in Figure 1.11, we would get something like this:

on(a,1,_)

on(b,1,_)

on(c,1,w(K))

on(d,1,w(R))

...

on(b,6,_)

on(c,6,b(N))

on(d,6,b(P))

...

and so on. Each square is represented by an expression consisting of a **predicate name** (in this case *on*) and three **arguments** (the symbols inside the brackets, separated by commas). The first argument represents the square's *column* (known as the *file* in chess jargon); the second represents the row (known as the *rank*); and the third gives the type of piece there. The piece is itself represented by a predicate name (w or b) and one argument (the kind of piece), with _ representing an empty square. As you read through this block, you'll find that this slightly odd-looking way of representing each simple fact is conventional in logic and AI.

Now we know how to represent the board, we need to think about how to represent the processes – the moves that pieces are legally capable of making. This is slightly more tricky, but once again there are plenty of possibilities. Each chess piece moves in its own particular way. For instance, the rook moves horizontally or vertically as far as you like, but must stop when reaching another piece (it can never leap over an occupied square). No piece, including the rook, may land on a square occupied by a piece of its own colour, but it is possible to move onto a square occupied by a piece of the opposite colour. This piece is then said to be *captured* and is removed from the board: Figure 1.13 illustrates these rules for the case of the rook.

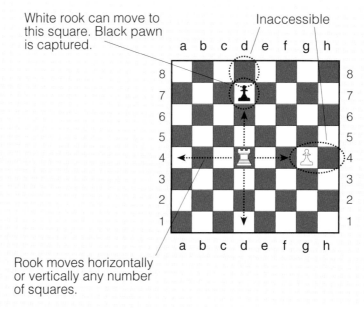

White rook can move to this square. Black pawn is captured.

Inaccessible

Rook moves horizontally or vertically any number of squares.

Figure 1.13   Legal moves of a rook

Taking the position shown in Figure 1.11, two of the expressions representing the state of the board at this point would be:

$on(d,1,w(R))$

$on(d,5,\_)$

Now suppose it is white's turn to move and he decides to move his rook on d1 to d5 (If you are an experienced chess player, you'll see this is a pretty suicidal move, but no matter.) The move will then alter these two expressions to:

$on(d,1,\_)$

$on(d,5,w(R))$

Quite simply, the effect of a move is to change the state of the board. And as you will recall from earlier, certain states are special. In games such as chess, and many other problems too, there is a *start state* and a *goal state*. In chess, there is only one start state (see Figure 1.14(a)). However, there may be many possible goal states. The aim of chess is to *checkmate* the opponent. The board is in a state of checkmate if a king is attacked by an enemy piece and cannot escape that attack, either by moving to any square where it would not be attacked or by capturing the attacking piece. Given that a king can legally move only one square in any direction, you can see that the black king in Figure 1.14(b) is checkmated. The white rook on g8 attacks the king. The king can only move to a7, b7 or b8, all of which are attacked by one of the rooks. The king cannot escape. This is checkmate, a goal state – the game is over.

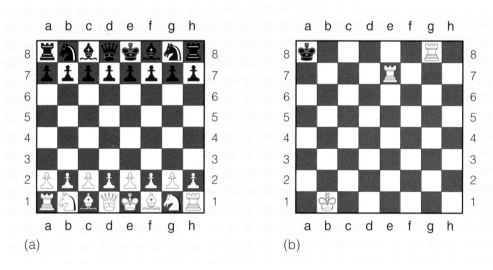

(a)   (b)

Figure 1.14   Sample chess positions: (a) opening position. (b) a checkmate position

Now it is quite easy to see in outline how a computerised chess program proceeds. In any board state S, including the start state, when it is the computer's turn to move the program simply goes through the following routine:

1   find which moves are legal in S;

2   choose the best move;

3   change the board state to the new state S';

4   check if a goal state has been found.

So really, playing chess is just a matter of selecting a series of moves that will lead to the goal state. Of course, a computer playing against a human does not know which moves its opponent will select, and so will have to reconsider its best move on each of its turns. But the problem is still just one of finding the best move from a given position, making it, and responding to the opponent's move until the goal state has been reached. Unfortunately, *representing* this simple-sounding process is incredibly problematic. The obvious approach is to have a large look-up table that contains every possible chess board configuration together with the best move from every state. However, there are quite a few chess positions and storing them all will take a lot of space.

Exercise 1.15

There around 10^{43} possible states of a chess game. If we assume that, on average, we would need six bits to store the location of each piece and there are an average of thirty-two pieces to store, how much storage space would it take to contain all these games? How large a hard disk would you require to store it? (At the time of writing, the best hard disks can pack around 20Gb onto one square centimetre.)

Discussion ....

We would need 192 bits = 24 bytes to store each position. Therefore, to hold all the reasonable games of chess, we need 24×10^{43} bytes to store the positions. A gigabyte is around 10^9 bytes, so the whole of chess requires 2.4×10^{35} Gb. Storing this much data would require a disk 1.2×10^{34} cm^2 = 1.2×10^{30} m^2 (for comparison, the surface area of the earth is around 5×10^{14} m^2). A 1.2×10^{30} m^2 disk has a radius 618 000 000 000 km, or about 4100 AU (astronomical units). This means that if it was centred on the Sun, the edge of the disk would be deep in interplanetary space, about 140 times more distant than Neptune.

And that's just to store the positions. If we want to record the best move for each, that requires another 143 bits per position. That means that we need a disk of around 816 000 000 000 km radius, 180 times that of Neptune's orbit.

Remember, these figures are only rough estimates. All I want you to take away from this exercise is the understanding that it is absolutely impossible for any conceivable computer to search systematically through all these possibilities. One way to avoid the computer having to sift through this immense space of possible games is to use special techniques of *heuristic search*, which I will discuss extensively in Unit 2.

Clearly humans don't play chess by searching through every possible position either. The representation for chess that we developed above is just adequate for the computer to play the most basic of games. However, there is a lot of evidence to suggest that expert *human* players, the men and women we call grandmasters, don't really think about the board just in this basic way. Although they do, of course, analyse positions, and the positions that might arise from them, very systematically, they generally see the positions in more abstract terms – in terms of *groups* of pieces in particular *patterns*. Here are two examples of such patterns:

▶ the *pin*: a piece is attacked but if it moves it exposes another piece to attack (see Figure 1.15(a));

▶ the *fork*: two pieces are attacked simultaneously (see Figure 1.15(b)).

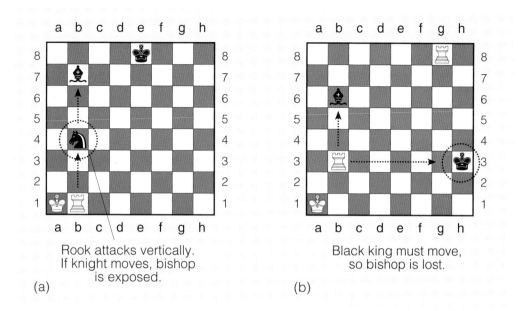

Rook attacks vertically.
If knight moves, bishop
is exposed.

(a)

Black king must move,
so bishop is lost.

(b)

Figure 1.15   Examples of pin and fork patterns in chess: (a) pin. (b) fork

This more abstract *knowledge* allows the players to reason about board positions more efficiently and to better predict the responses to a sequence of moves. If we want to take advantage of this higher level knowledge, we need to form some kind of representation for it. However, we will obviously always need the sort of basic representation I've developed here, to determine what moves are legal and how to translate our high level objectives into low level individual piece moves.

7.2 | Expert systems

As I mentioned at the very start of this unit, a hallmark of intelligence is often taken to be the behaviour of *experts* when solving problems in their domain of expertise. The best chess-playing programs are, to a limited extent, modelled on the grandmasters' understanding of the game. One particular breed of intelligent system, known as **expert systems**, is designed to capture the behaviour of skilled specialists. Expert systems have been one of the great success stories of Symbolic AI. An expert system captures an expert's knowledge about a specialised domain and uses that knowledge to solve problems in that domain automatically. It generally has two main components: the *knowledge base* and the *inference engine* (see Figure 1.16).

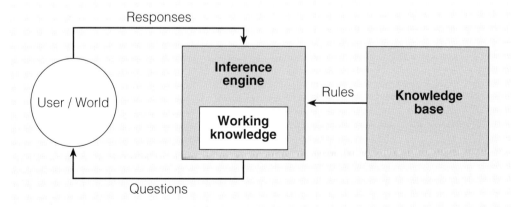

Figure 1.16   Architecture of an expert system

Consider an expert system designed to assist with car maintenance and fault finding. The knowledge base would contain the expert knowledge, often as a set of **production rules** such as:

```
IF NOT engine-turns-over
   AND NOT headlights-are-bright
THEN problem-with-battery
```

These rules can be used for **inference**, where new knowledge is discovered about a situation. For instance, the rule above is able to determine whether the battery in a car is flat. The rule is in two parts: the **antecedent** or **premise** (everything between the IF and the THEN) and the **consequent** or **conclusion** (everything after the THEN). If the inference process can show that the antecedent is true, then the consequent is also true. When a rule is used to prove its consequent, that rule is said to **fire**. As well as being used to derive new knowledge in this way, rules can also suggest actions to perform, or questions to ask the user in certain situations (such as asking the user to turn on the headlights and see how bright they are). I will return to this distinction in Section 8.1.

The extent of the system's expertise is determined by the size of its knowledge base. A dozen rules may be all that is needed to give the expert system some rudimentary expertise; a few dozen may contain sufficient knowledge to cope with common and simple problems. But this is generally woefully inadequate for genuine, wide-ranging expert performance, so 'industrial strength' expert systems typically have thousands of rules, distilled from the knowledge of batteries of human experts.

The inference engine, as its name suggests, is the part of the expert system that does the reasoning. Inference may start with some initial information (if any) about the situation and perhaps a goal that we want the system to achieve. In the car diagnosis example, the system's goal is to identify what is wrong with the car, but it probably knows nothing about the car at the start. The inference engine's task is to consult the knowledge base and use the rules there to deduce new knowledge based on what it has deduced so far, and from information from the user: for instance, the user may have told the system that the car engine does not turn over. What the expert system currently knows about this situation is stored as *working knowledge* in the inference engine.

The inference engine may very quickly run out of things to derive from its existing knowledge. When this happens, it will have to ask the user further questions in order to gain new facts. Using the example rule above, the inference engine may determine that it should ask about the state of the headlights, so it will generate a question and put it to the user. After the user determines the answer to the question (by turning on the lights and looking at them) and giving the response, the inference system adds this new fact to its working knowledge (often together with the fact that it has now asked about the lights) and uses this new fact to derive new knowledge (such as the battery being flat).

SAQ 1.6

Why would the expert system want to record that it has asked a question?

ANSWER...

To prevent the expert system asking the same question again, such as when the fact it relates to appears in another rule it is processing.

However, things are generally not that simple. Most of the time, there will be *several* rules that could be used for the next reasoning step, and the inference engine must choose between them. This is termed **conflict resolution**. There are many ways of achieving conflict resolution, which I won't go into here. The important point is that only one rule can be used at a time, and the inference engine has to use some form of knowledge to choose between them. I will discuss this in Section 8.1.

Several facts may be marked as being goals of the expert system. If any of these facts appears in the knowledge base, the system has achieved its aim and its work can stop. In the example rule above, the fact `problem-with-battery` could have been designated as a goal, as determining that the battery is flat would be a successful diagnosis of the problem with the car. If the aim of the expert system was to fix the car as well, the goal would be the fact `car-is-running`.

An additional facility that most expert systems have is the ability to 'explain their reasoning'. From the user's perspective, a consultation with an expert system is a question-and-answer session, with the system asking the user for facts and the user supplying them. Since most people are little inclined to trust machines, especially with delicate matters, at any point in this dialogue the user should be able to ask the expert system 'Why are you asking me this question?' or 'How do you know this to be true?' and should be given the relevant explanation. You can see how this works in the sample dialogue in Box 1.3.

Box 1.3: Expert system dialogue

```
Are the headlights dim?
> why?
I am trying to discover if the car battery is flat.
By rule 37, if the engine does not turn over and the headlights are
dim then the battery is flat.
I know the engine does not turn over because: you told me so.
Are the headlights dim?
> yes
The battery is flat.
> how?
Because rule 37 says that if the engine does not turn over and the
headlights are dim then the battery is flat.
I know the engine does not turn over because: you told me so.
I know the headlights are dim because: you told me so.
```

8 Representation

Now that you have met some of the basic concepts of symbolic reasoning systems, it is time to consider them in more detail. In this section, I will look at a few representation systems, describe what they are used for, assess their strengths and weaknesses, and examine the trade-offs to be made between them. In the next section, I shall discuss how to reason with these representations. But before I get to that, I need to clarify what these representations are actually *representing*: I need to say something about *knowledge*.

8.1 Types of knowledge

Throughout our discussions so far, the topic of 'knowledge' has popped up many times. Indeed, it is an idea that is central to the Symbolic AI approach. Following on from Exercise 1.2 in Section 2, you will have noticed that the word 'knowledge' is used in different ways in different situations. For instance, in the discussion of expert systems in Section 7.2, I distinguished between knowledge of *facts* (such as the faults that were present in the car) and *actions* (such as how to fix the problems). In this I will try to tease out and explain some of these different uses.

We are going to make three key distinctions between types of knowledge:

▶ between facts and actions;

▶ between declarative and procedural knowledge;

▶ between base knowledge and meta-knowledge;

and discuss each of these in turn.

Facts and actions

The difference between **facts** and **actions** is one of the deepest assumptions of the physical symbol system hypothesis (see Section 4). Recall that the PSSH posits that an intelligent system is composed of symbol expressions that both designate objects and represent processes that can be interpreted to change the state of the physical symbol system.

If we are to create intelligent systems that act in the world, we need to be able to have them both reason about the state of the world, perhaps inferring events from observable features, and decide on what actions to take. The expert system in our example above did just that. Therefore, the system needs representations of both facts and actions. Our expert system example used the same representation (such as the production rules) for both, interpreting the conclusion of a rule as either a fact to add to its working knowledge or an action to perform. Representing knowledge in this unitary way makes the system's internal representation cleaner, and may be an easy form in which the human domain expert's knowledge can be expressed. However, a unified approach can lead to confused inference, as there are situations in which the system may have to decide whether the conclusion of a rule is a new fact or an action to perform.

Declarative and procedural knowledge

Another distinction we can draw between different types of knowledge arises from how it can be encoded. Some knowledge is (or can be) explicitly stated, such as the knowledge that my cup of tea is empty. I can write down such knowledge in an unambiguous form that I can show to another person and thus communicate easily. This is called **declarative knowledge** (sometimes called **know-that knowledge**). Declarative knowledge is obviously useful in intelligent systems: if we can make an explicit declaration of some item of knowledge, we can encode it neatly in some form of representation, turning it straightforwardly into a symbol expression that designates that knowledge. This is true whether the expression designates a fact, an object or a process: if we can point to a symbol expression that encodes some knowledge, that knowledge is declarative.

Other knowledge, such as my knowledge of how to juggle, cannot be written down, and it is very difficult to pass that knowledge from person to person. Knowledge of how to juggle, or ride a bike, or speak French is still *knowledge*: we quite happily speak of someone knowing how to juggle, or learning how to drive, etc. But it does seem to be a different kind of knowledge, termed **procedural knowledge**, as it is expressed in the procedures that an intelligent agent performs, the behaviour it exhibits. Procedural knowledge is also known as implicit, tacit or **know-how knowledge**. Arguably, procedural knowledge is much more a factor in intelligent behaviour than declarative knowledge: we know how to do countless things, none of which we can confidently explain to another person.

SAQ 1.7

Write down three other examples of declarative and procedural knowledge.

ANSWER...

Your list will certainly be different from mine, but some examples of declarative knowledge I came up with include a recipe in a cookery book, the expression for the roots of a quadratic equation

$$x = \frac{-b \pm \sqrt{b^2 - 4ac}}{2a}$$

and the declaration of the difference between declarative and procedural knowledge. Some examples of procedural knowledge are knowing how to cook a familiar dish, knowing how to drive and knowing how to read.

There is a significant problem with procedural knowledge when it comes to developing intelligent systems: how do we represent it? It is relatively easy to represent declarative knowledge as a set of symbolic expressions, but if we want to include procedural knowledge in an intelligent system (and we will almost certainly have to), we have to decide on a representation system of some kind. This is essentially the problem that infant school teachers face daily (try writing an algorithm for tying shoelaces or opening all the myriad types of door you encounter). And if humans find communicating procedural knowledge to other humans difficult, we can only expect it to be much more difficult when we have to explain things to a computer.

We could take the view that as declarative knowledge is easy to represent and hence easy to reason about, so we should only include (so far as is possible) declarative knowledge in our system. But this is impractical and just avoids the problem. Another way of side-stepping the issue is to keep the procedural knowledge implicit in the system we're building and design the system in such a way that the desired behaviour arises from interactions inside it. In this case, we say that the procedural knowledge is an *emergent property* of the system: emergence is one of the core concepts of M366 and is introduced in Block 3. But, given the difficulty of designing and implementing emergent behaviours, Symbolic AI has traditionally focused on declarative knowledge.

Another reason why designing and implementing procedural knowledge has been less popular than encoding it as declarative knowledge is that there is less scope for reasoning about that knowledge. This brings us to the third distinction we can draw between types of knowledge.

Base knowledge and meta-knowledge

The final distinction between types of knowledge that I will discuss here is between **base knowledge** (also known as object knowledge or domain knowledge) and **meta-knowledge**. Put simply, base knowledge is a system's knowledge about a domain, while meta-knowledge is knowledge about that knowledge. For instance, car mechanics may know how to diagnose a faulty car (base knowledge), but they are likely also to be able to say that they are *capable* of making such a diagnosis. Such a statement about their own knowledge is *meta-knowledge*: knowledge about their knowledge.

The examples I have looked at so far in this unit contain several examples of meta-knowledge. In our chess-playing example (see Section 7.1), the base knowledge concerns the rules of the game, such as the allowable moves and the definition of checkmate. Concepts such as pins and forks are still base knowledge, although at a more abstract level, dealing as they do with collections of pieces. In contrast, meta-knowledge is knowledge about this knowledge, and concerns things like knowing what board positions are good or bad and the broad strategies, such as taking control of the centre of the board. Meta-knowledge of this kind can be used to guide the player's reasoning to explore the promising moves while quickly disregarding the bad ones. In the expert system example (see Section 7.2), the base knowledge lies in the production rules and the basic inference processes for diagnosing faults.

SAQ 1.8

Would you say an expert system has any meta-knowledge? If so, what is it?

ANSWER...

An expert system has some meta-knowledge. Specifically, it has knowledge about what it's trying to do and why it's going about it in the way it is. This meta-knowledge is revealed in its answers to 'how' and 'why' questions. You should also note that the expert system I described *lacks* certain elements of meta-knowledge: the system does not know when a particular problem lies outside its domain of expertise, for example. This can lead to problems if the system is used inappropriately: it will have no way of recognising when its base knowledge is inapplicable and its answers thus become meaningless.

From these examples, we can see that meta-knowledge performs two roles in an intelligent system:

▶ It makes it possible for the system to reason about what it is doing and how it is doing it. This is called **meta-reasoning**. For instance, a chess player may know that a particular move will set up an attack later, or a car diagnosis expert system may know that flat batteries are a common fault and so should be investigated before other possibilities such as water in the fuel tank. Therefore, meta-knowledge helps the system identify the best way to achieve the tasks it is faced with. It also gives the system the flexibility to change its problem-solving approach depending on the situation: for instance, changing from forward to backward reasoning (see Section 9.1).

▶   Meta-knowledge allows the system to state its own capabilities, and therefore reason about them. This is important when we put an intelligent agent into the world, which will be populated with other agents (whether intelligent or not, and including people), tools, etc. It allows the system to choose which problems it should deal with, which it needs help with, and how it can help others.

SAQ 1.9

Briefly describe the difference between declarative and procedural knowledge and between base knowledge and meta-knowledge.

ANSWER...

Declarative knowledge is knowledge that can be explicitly declared, for instance by writing down. Procedural knowledge is knowledge that can only be expressed by performing a task.

Base knowledge is knowledge about a domain. Meta-knowledge is knowledge about knowledge, such as how to go about a task or how to state one's own capabilities.

Exercise 1.16

Let's revisit the interior design problem of Section 3.1. Assume that you're trying to develop a computer system that can generate arrangements of furniture in a room. Your system will use a CAD engine to keep track of the geometry of the room and the arrangement of the furniture in it. You can tell the CAD engine to place an item in a certain position and orientation in the room. You can also ask the CAD engine questions about the room, such as where a given item is, whether one piece of furniture intersects with another (or a wall), the size of gaps, routes from one position to another, and so on.

Given this set of base knowledge, what meta-knowledge would you need to create a useful and pleasing arrangement of furniture?

Discussion ....

Recall that meta-knowledge comes in two types. The first type, which allows the system to reason about what it's doing, is important in this example. The objective is 'to create a useful and pleasing arrangement of furniture', so the terms 'useful' and 'pleasing' need to be defined and to be measurable somehow. For instance, the 'usefulness' score of a chest of drawers may depend on how much space there is in front of it. Similarly, a room may be judged more 'pleasing' the greater the empty space in the middle. Other meta-knowledge might guide the system in its problem-solving procedures, such as the knowledge that it's often better to place the largest item of furniture first.

The second type of meta-knowledge is a system's knowledge of its own capabilities. This is unlikely to be as important in this situation, as the room organiser is probably not expected to interact with other agents. However, such a capacity could be useful if we wanted the system to explain its reasoning for proposing a given layout.

Exercise 1.17

In Section 2, in Exercise 1.2, I asked you to note, during your reading, the different ways the term 'knowledge' is referred to in this unit. The discussion above is my view on the different ways 'knowledge' has been used in AI. How do these categorisations correspond to the ones you've developed?

8.2 | What makes a good representation?

Now we know the sort of things we have to represent in an intelligent system, we can start to develop structures for representing them. I will develop some examples in Section 8.3, but before we get there, we first need to look at the desiderata of any representation we develop. This will give us criteria for judging whether the representational schemes we develop are good ones or not, and which can guide any trade-offs we may have to make. The features of a good representation include:

▶ *Coverage.* The representation should allow all the important elements of the problem to be described. For instance, a representational scheme for a chess-playing system should cover, at a minimum, the squares on the board and the pieces (including type and colour) occupying them. Often, identifying all the factors to include in a representation is not easy, particularly when dealing with complex domains. However, if the representation is incomplete, the intelligent system will not be able to perform properly, let alone perform well.

▶ *Parsimony* . While the representation must contain all the knowledge that is necessary, it should not contain anything unnecessary. Most interesting problems are complex, and an intelligent system will have a hard enough time choosing between the relevant choices it faces. If the space of possible decisions is made greater by the inclusion of irrelevant factors, the performance of the system will suffer. The wider the choice of actions, the more processing time will be needed to consider them.

This principle of parsimony also applies to representations that make irrelevant distinctions between states of affairs. For instance, in chess, the precise location of a piece within a square does not matter and so should not be included in the representation of a chess-playing program (although it might be needed in a chess-playing robot that is expected to manipulate the physical pieces directly).

▶ *Clarity.* A good representation should make clear how it represents the world. This allows for an easy translation from a statement of the problem (in English, say) to the symbolic expressions that represent it. This is especially useful when the system needs to explain its actions. A clear representation also makes the development of the system easier, as the developer can see more simply what the knowledge is supposed to represent.

▶ *Use of derived knowledge.* In many domains, knowledge can be derived from existing facts. For instance, in chess, whether a king is in 'check' or not can be worked out simply from the positions of the various pieces on the board. Storing such knowledge explicitly may reduce the computational load – it will not have to be derived every time it is needed; but it will have to be recreated every time the situation changes. Determining how much of the knowledge could be derived, and how much should be stated explicitly instead, is an engineering decision.

▶ *Specificity.* There is a large number of existing symbolic notations that can be used to represent problems, a few of which I will discuss in Section 8.3. For instance, we could adopt predicate logic or production rules, or even develop our own special-purpose representation, such as the one I used for the mutilated chessboard puzzle. The advantage of reusing an existing notation is that many tools and results have already been developed for it. For this reason, predicate logic is often used as a notation for expressing knowledge, because it is easy to build inference mechanisms that use it and its properties are well known. The disadvantage of general-purpose representational systems such as predicate logic is that they are quite low-level, and substantial work may be required to ensure full coverage.

On the other hand, if we use a representation that is developed specifically for the task at hand, we can be certain that its features match that task. The disadvantage is that we will have to build efficient reasoning systems specifically for it.

No representation will be perfect and all representations will fulfil these five criteria to a greater or lesser extent. The art of the designer of an intelligent system is to weigh up the various criteria with respect to the tasks the system should perform, and then select the representation that provides the best match. The next section gives an overview of a few standard representation schemes.

Exercise 1.18

In Sections 5 and 7, I outlined possible representational schemes for several problems (water jugs, missionaries and cannibals, chess, expert reasoning). Evaluate each of those representations against the five criteria described above.

Discussion ....

I've shown my evaluation in Table 1.2.

As you can see, there are differences between the features of the representations. Simple representations for simple problems (water jugs, missionaries and cannibals are very close to the problem. This means they work efficiently for that problem, but are not adaptable. Representations for more complex problems, such as chess and car diagnosis, are themselves more complex. However, they can often be modified to deal with other problems.

Table 1.2 Evaluation of four problems according to the five criteria for a good representation

	Water jugs	Missionaries and cannibals	Chess	Expert reasoning
Representation	Amount of water in the jugs.	Number of missionaries, cannibals and boats on each bank.	Contents of each square.	Production rules.
Coverage	Complete: nothing else in the problem that needs to be specified.	Complete: nothing else in the problem that needs to be specified.	Also need to record whose turn it is. How much time is available to each player may also influence decision making.	Only simple and definite knowledge can be expressed. Default knowledge, degrees of certainty cannot be represented.
Parsimony	Includes some states that are unreachable from the starting position (such as the three-litre jug holding two litres while the four-litre jug holds three litres), but this is only a problem if all the states are explicitly generated at first.	Includes some states that are unreachable from the starting position (such as three missionaries and three cannibals on the left bank, with the boat on the right), but this is only a problem if all the states are explicitly generated at first.	The given representation also includes describing the empty squares: this isn't strictly needed.	In most cases, the knowledge base will contain rules that are never used for a particular consultation. The problem is predicting which rules will not be needed for any consultation!

Table continues over page

	Water jugs	Missionaries and cannibals	Chess	Expert reasoning
Clarity	The representation is fairly clear, once you know what it's for. There is a possibility of confusion in whether the contents of the larger jug are listed first or second.	The representation is fairly clear, once you know what it's for. There is a possibility of confusion in whether the number of missionaries is listed first or second.	The representation is clear, so long as you know the codes for the pieces and the coordinate system used for the board.	Individual rules are clear (but could become less so if they become big) but the overall knowledge base could become too large to comprehend.
Derived knowledge	No useful derived knowledge.	The occupants of the right bank can be derived from the initial state and who's missing from the left bank. This is needed to check if anyone gets eaten.	As described in Section 7.1, there are many features of chess positions (open files, etc.) that aren't represented directly. These have to be derived from the representation if they are to be used.	No scope for derived knowledge: everything must be explicit, derived from the rules.
Specificity	This representation can only be used for this type of problem.	This representation can only be used for this type of problem.	The notion of recording the contents of a square on a board can be used for all manner of board games (draughts, ludo, Risk, etc.).	Production rules can be used for a variety of purposes, generally where some form of deduction is the key part of the problem.

8.3 Examples of representations

Now that we've seen a variety of representations and outlined principles that can help determine whether a representation is good or bad, it's time to take a brief look at some of the more popular representational schemes – sometimes called **formalisms** – used in Symbolic AI. As you've discovered in tackling some of the exercises, developing new representations is hard, especially when the problem is complex and there are different types of reasoning to be done. For this reason, many general-purpose representations have been developed. As I've suggested, these can be adapted to a variety of problem areas with much less effort than it takes to create a new representation from scratch. In this section, I'll take a look at some of the more popular formalisms and discuss their strengths and weaknesses.

Symbolic logic

Computer scientists have had a long relationship with symbolic logic. It started with George Boole's publication in 1847 of his 'laws of thought' and this has continued, through the work of Frege, Russell and Turing, to the present day. The core idea of symbolic logic is to develop an algebra for *truth*, similar to the more familiar algebra for numeric values. Logical expressions are used to represent facts in the world and the rules of the logic are used to derive new facts from the existing ones. There are numerous types of symbolic logic, varying in how they represent facts and what inference rules they use. However, I am only going to outline two of the most widely used logics here: propositional logic and first-order predicate logic.

In **propositional logic** (also called **propositional calculus**) each symbol in a logical expression represents a fact, or **proposition**. For instance, the symbol R may represent the proposition 'it is raining', the symbol U represents the proposition 'I am carrying an umbrella' and W represents 'I am wet'. These propositions can be combined using the logical connectives such as '$\wedge$' and '$\neg$' (see Table 1.3) to produce *sentences* of propositional logic, such as $R \wedge U$. This logical sentence means 'it is raining and I am carrying an umbrella' and it is true exactly when both of its propositions are true.

Table 1.3 Logical connectives

Connective	Meaning	Alternative term
$\wedge$	And	Conjunction
$\vee$	Or	Disjunction
$\neg$	Not	Negation
$\rightarrow$	Implies (if)	
$\leftrightarrow$	Equivalent (if and only if)	

Note that in Table 1.3, both 'implies' and 'equivalent' are logical connectives, not rules of inference.

SAQ 1.10

What are the meanings of $R \vee U$ and $\neg W$?

ANSWER...

It is raining *or* I am carrying an umbrella; I am not wet.

Sentences can be made up from other sentences and connectives, such as $(R \wedge U) \rightarrow \neg W$ ('If it's raining and I've got my umbrella then I'm not wet'). Table 1.4 shows the truth tables for the connectives; they show when a sentence is true or false depending on the truth values of its components. The truth table for a sentence can be built up from the truth tables of its components. If two sentences have the same truth table, we say they are equivalent (i.e. they are both true under exactly the same circumstances).

Table 1.4 Truth tables of the logical connectives

A	B	$A \wedge B$	$A \vee B$	$\neg A$	$A \rightarrow B$	$A \leftrightarrow B$
False	False	False	False	True	True	True
False	True	False	True	True	True	False
True	False	False	True	False	False	False
True	True	True	True	False	True	True

Inference is done by applying defined **rules of inference**, such as those listed in Table 1.5. By adopting different rules of inference, we can define different logics; however those in Table 1.5 are commonly used as they match our understanding of logical reasoning in the real world. We can use these rules to infer new propositions from given ones. An example is in Table 1.6 where I derive the fact of my dryness from the **axioms** given in the first three lines of the derivation. In this case, we say that my being not wet is **entailed** by the axioms given.

Table 1.5 Rules of inference in propositional logic

Name of rule	Expression	Meaning
Modus ponens	$$\dfrac{\alpha \rightarrow \beta \quad \alpha}{\beta}$$	Given an implication and its premise, infer the conclusion
And elimination	$$\dfrac{\alpha_1 \wedge \alpha_2 \wedge ... \wedge \alpha_n}{\alpha_i}$$	Given a conjunction, infer one of the conjuncts
And introduction	$$\dfrac{\alpha_1 \quad \alpha_2 \quad ... \quad \alpha_n}{\alpha_1 \wedge \alpha_2 \wedge ... \wedge \alpha_n}$$	Given a set of sentences, infer their conjunction
Or introduction	$$\dfrac{\alpha_1 \quad \alpha_2 \quad ... \quad \alpha_n}{\alpha_1 \vee \alpha_2 \vee ... \vee \alpha_n}$$	Given a set of sentences, infer their disjunction
Double negation elimination	$$\dfrac{\neg\neg\alpha}{\alpha}$$	If something is not false, infer that it is true
Unit resolution	$$\dfrac{\alpha \vee \beta \quad \neg\beta}{\alpha}$$	Given a disjunction and that one of the disjuncts is false, infer the other
Resolution	$$\dfrac{\alpha \vee \beta \quad \neg\beta \vee \gamma}{\alpha \vee \gamma}$$	β cannot be both true and false, so one of the disjuncts in the other sentences must be true

Table 1.6 An example inference

Line	Proposition	Comments
1	R	Axiom
2	U	Axiom
3	$(R \wedge U) \rightarrow \neg W$	Axiom
4	$R \wedge U$	1, 2, and introduction
5	$\neg W$	4, 3, modus ponens

Exercise 1.19

Many parts of this discussion of symbolic logic should have been familiar to you from your understanding of the physical symbol system hypothesis. Draw up a list of the main features of physical symbol systems and state what elements of symbolic logic you think correspond to them.

Discussion ....

The list of features for physical symbol systems comes from Activity 1.1. As you can see from Table 1.7, the two sets of features are very similar. This shouldn't be a big surprise, as the formulation of the PSSH was based on work in symbolic logic.

Table 1.7

Physical symbol systems	Propositional logic
Symbol expressions designate objects.	Propositions designate states of affairs.
Symbol expressions are used to represent symbol manipulation processes.	Rules of inference are explicitly stated (see Table 1.5).
Processing occurs by manipulating symbol expressions according to the processes defined.	Deduction takes place by manipulating the set of propositions according to the defined rules of inference.

Propositional logic is simple, but unfortunately it is not expressive enough to represent everything we routinely want to, such as sentences like 'All men are mortal.' It also can't express the fact that the people referred to by the propositions U and W above are the same. **Predicate logic** (also called predicate calculus) allows us to state sentences like this. Predicate logic sees the world as collections of objects that have properties and relations with other objects; objects are different from each other because they have different properties (such as names). The logic uses symbols to represent objects (such as *Neil* and *Socrates*) and **predicates** (such as *mortal* and *wet*) to pick out properties of objects and relations between them. For example, the predicate *mortal(Socrates)* is true exactly when the object *Socrates* is mortal, and *writing(Neil,M366)* is true exactly when there is a *writing* relationship between *Neil* and *M366* (i.e. when I'm writing materials for this course). Predicates can be defined with any number of objects as arguments but a predicate with, say, two arguments may have a quite different meaning from the same predicate with three, so the meaning must be defined in each case. You might remember that this *predicate(arguments)* structure is the one I used in Section 7.1 to represent board states in chess.

Sentences in predicate logic can be built up using the same connectives as for propositional logic; the same rules of inference apply too. The predicate nature of the logic is exploited by using **quantifiers** that allow us to say things about whole classes of objects. Predicate logic has two quantifiers, the **universal quantifier** (written $\forall$) and the **existential quantifier** (written $\exists$). When we use these quantifiers, we also need to introduce variables into the logic sentences and the quantifiers range over these variables. For example, in the predicate logic sentence $\forall x \; man(x) \rightarrow mortal(x)$ the quantifier ranges over the variable x. The universal quantifier means 'for every' or 'for all'; so, translated into English, the expression means, roughly, 'for all x, if x is a man, then x is mortal'.

When we use a universal quantifier, the sentence is true only if it would remain true whatever value we substitute for the variable. In other words, $\forall x \; man(x) \rightarrow mortal(x)$ is true if and only if $man(Neil) \rightarrow mortal(Neil)$ is true, $man(Socrates) \rightarrow mortal(Socrates)$ is true and $man(MyDesk) \rightarrow mortal(MyDesk)$ is true. If every substitution of x in the quantified sentence would make the substituted sentence true, then the quantified sentence $\forall x \; man(x) \rightarrow mortal(x)$ is true also.

SAQ 1.11

Use the truth tables in Table 1.4 to check for yourself that the sentence $man(MyDesk) \rightarrow mortal(MyDesk)$ is true.

ANSWER..

Refer back to the truth tables in Table 1.4. Both *man*(*MyDesk*) and *mortal*(*MyDesk*) are false, so the sentence itself is true.

The existential quantifier means 'there exists'. When we use an existential quantifier, the sentence is true if we can find at least one value for the variable that would make the sentence true. For example, the sentence $\exists x\ hasPet(Neil,x) \land cat(x)$ ('Neil has a pet cat') is true if we can find some x that satisfies both parts of the conjunction. Substituting *Socrates* for x doesn't fit the bill, but substituting *Schrödinger* for x results in a true sentence. We write such a substitution as *Subst*(x/*Schrödinger*,*hasPet*(*Neil*,x)): we substitute *Schrödinger* for x in the sentence *hasPet*(*Neil*,x), giving the sentence *hasPet*(*Neil*,*Schrödinger*) ('Neil has a pet cat called Schrödinger').

The rules of inference for predicate logic are all those we could use for propositional logic, plus a few more to cope with quantifiers (see Table 1.8).

Table 1.8 Inference rules for predicate logic

Name of rule	Expression	Meaning
Universal elimination	$$\dfrac{\forall v\ \alpha}{Subst(v\,/\,g,\alpha)}$$	For example, from $\forall x\ mortal(x)$ we can substitute *Neil* for x and infer *mortal*(*Neil*).
Existential elimination	$$\dfrac{\exists v\ \alpha}{Subst(v\,/\,k,\alpha)}$$	For example, from $\exists x\ mother(x,Neil)$ we can substitute *Gina* for x and infer *mother*(*Gina*,*Neil*).
Existential introduction	$$\dfrac{\alpha}{\exists v\ Subst(g\,/\,v,\alpha)}$$	For example, from *mother*(*Gina*,*Neil*) we can substitute x for *Gina* and infer $\exists x\ mother(x,Neil)$.

Note: v is a variable, g is a ground term (a term that contains no variables), k is a term that does not occur elsewhere, α is any sentence.

I've spent a while describing symbolic logic; now it's time to discuss its usefulness as a representation method. Symbolic logic has three main advantages over other possible representations of problems:

▶ It has a very strict formal syntax and semantics, which means that there can be no confusion or vagueness about what's being stated in the representation.

▶ It has been in use for over 150 years so its properties are well known. These properties include things like the reliability of reasoning and the cost of the inference procedures.

▶ As you discovered in Exercise 1.19, it is very close to the formal properties of physical symbol systems and therefore the mapping from the representation to the machine that will use it is easy.

However, it has some problems as a representation. Symbolic logic is a very low-level way of stating facts about the world and it typically requires dozens, if not hundreds, of expressions to be stated before any useful work can be done, as the exercise below shows.

Exercise 1.20

Spend a few minutes thinking about how you would represent the missionaries-and-cannibals problem in predicate logic. You need to think about how to represent a state as well as how to represent the transitions between states.

Discussion ....

We could use the approach of pure predicate logic and have one symbol for each missionary and cannibal. However, the easier way is to exploit the interchangeability of the missionaries and cannibals and simply record the number of each on each bank. This gives us a representation very close to the one described in Section 5.

We can represent the state of the world with a single predicate, *on_left_bank*(*m,c,b*), which records the number of missionaries, cannibals and boats on the left bank. We can also define a predicate *anyone_eaten?*(*m,c*) which is true if the cannibals have eaten any missionaries. The definition of *anyone_eaten?* is:

anyone_eaten?(*m,c*) ↔ ($c > m \land m > 0$) ∨ ($c < m \land m < 3$)

We can define a predicate *possible_move(m0,c0,b0,m,c,b)* that is true when the move from *on_left_bank(m0,c0,b0)* to *on_left_bank(m,c,b)* is possible:

possible_move(m0,c0,b0,m,c,b) ↔
   ($b0 > 0 \land m0 \geq 1 \land b = b0 - 1 \land m = m0 - 1$) ∨
   ($b0 > 0 \land m0 \geq 2 \land b = b0 - 1 \land m = m0 - 2$) ∨
   ($b0 > 0 \land m0 \geq 1 \land c0 \geq 1 \land b = b0 - 1 \land m = m0 - 1 \land c = c0 - 1$) ∨
   ($b0 > 0 \land c0 \geq 1 \land b = b0 - 1 \land c = c0 - 1$) ∨
   ($b0 > 0 \land c0 \geq 2 \land b = b0 - 1 \land c = c0 - 2$) ∨
   ($b0 < 1 \land m0 \leq 2 \land b = b0 + 1 \land m = m0 + 1$) ∨
   ($b0 < 1 \land m0 \leq 1 \land b = b0 + 1 \land m = m0 + 2$) ∨
   ($b0 < 1 \land m0 \leq 2 \land c0 \leq 2 \land b = b0 + 1 \land m = m0 + 1 \land c = c0 + 1$) ∨
   ($b0 < 1 \land c0 \leq 2 \land b = b0 + 1 \land c = c0 + 1$) ∨
   ($b0 < 1 \land c0 \leq 1 \land b = b0 + 1 \land c = c0 + 2$)

Finally, we can define a *legal_move* as being a possible move where no one gets eaten:

legal_move(m0,c0,b0,m,c,b) ↔
   possible_move(m0,c0,b0,m,c,b) ∧
   ¬ (*anyone_eaten?*(*m0,c0*) ∨ *anyone_eaten?*(*m,c*))

We also need to define predicates for start and goal:

start (*3,3,1*)

goal (*0,0,0*)

We're now at the stage where we have a full representation of the problem. However, we still need to put together the apparatus that will find a solution to the problem, by generating a set of possible moves, finding which is the best one, updating the state of the world, and detecting whether we've reached a goal state. This is the subject of Unit 2.

I hope that this little exercise has given you an insight into the number of predicates needed to describe even a very simple problem.

Symbolic logic is rarely used directly in practical Symbolic AI systems: it's too verbose to allow much useful work to be done. However, it serves well as a *lingua franca* into which other formalisms can be translated, allowing them to be compared with each other. Other representational schemes may also be able to reuse some of the symbolic logic's results.

Semantic networks

As I've argued, one of the drawbacks of logic-based representations is their verbosity. Another is that they can't really take account of any *structure* in the knowledge being represented. These drawbacks can be overcome by representing knowledge with a **semantic network**, a formalism similar in many ways to the conventional data structures in computer science. A semantic network represents a set of entities and relationships between them. The entities can be either objects, collections of objects, or concepts.

There are several types of semantic network. The two most widely used are **definitional networks** (which define concepts in terms of other concepts) and **assertional networks** (which describe sets of assertions or propositions, rather like the predicate logic examples given above). Figure 1.17 shows a semantic network that defines the concepts Truck and TrailerTruck as subtypes of Vehicle.

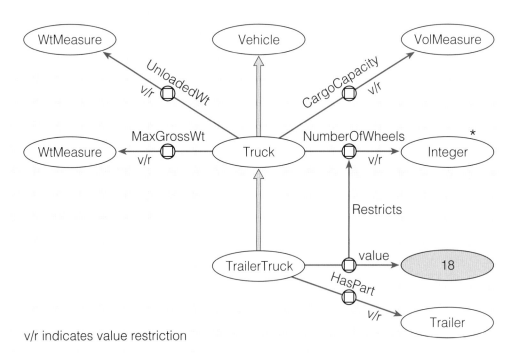

v/r indicates value restriction

Figure 1.17   Definition of Truck and TrailerTruck concepts

The ovals represent concepts that are relevant to trucks. All these concepts can take on the value of a specific truck, apart from the one represented by the shaded oval, which restricts the number of wheels for all TrailerTrucks to 18. The asterisk marking the 'Integer' oval indicates that this concept is of a primitive (built-in) type. The other concepts in the diagram (Vehicle, Trailer, WtMeasure and VolMeasure) would need to be defined elsewhere in the semantic network.

The broad arrows represent subtype–supertype links from TrailerTruck to Truck and from Truck to Vehicle: a Truck is a type of Vehicle, and a TrailerTruck is a type of Truck. The arrows with a circle in the middle represent roles that these concepts play in the definition of the Truck concept; they are similar to attributes of the Truck. For instance, a Truck has a CargoCapacity that is a VolMeasure. The TrailerTruck node has two roles, one labelled HasPart (a TrailerTruck has a Trailer as a part) and one that restricts the NumberOfWheels role of Truck to the value 18. The notation v/r on a role arrow indicates a value restriction, a limit on the permissible values for those roles.

Frames and scripts

When we think about the natural world, we make a lot of inferences based on how we expect things to work. For instance, if we hear of a bird, we naturally assume that the bird has various characteristics, such as having feathers, being able to fly, and so on. Normally, it's only when those assumptions are in danger of being wrong that they are even mentioned: Tweety may not need an aviary if Tweety is an ostrich. This human ability to bring default knowledge to bear on a situation led to the development of two similar representations: frames and scripts.

Frames share many similarities with semantic networks. However, frames are specialised to deal with *taxonomies*. Each frame represents an object, as in a semantic network, and has a name and a number of **slots** that contain information about that object. The slots are attribute–value pairs; the attributes are the slot names and the values are the slot fillers. The most common links between slots are termed *is_a* links and represent inheritance. For instance, in Figure 1.18, a bird *is_a* animal and an ostrich *is_a* bird. Where a frame does not contain a value for a particular slot, that value is inherited from its ancestor frame. This allows the frame system to rely on default values for slots except where they are overridden by more specific information.

The notion of storing data in discrete objects that inherit data and methods from their ancestors in a taxonomic hierarchy was adopted by software developers and became the object-oriented programming paradigm.

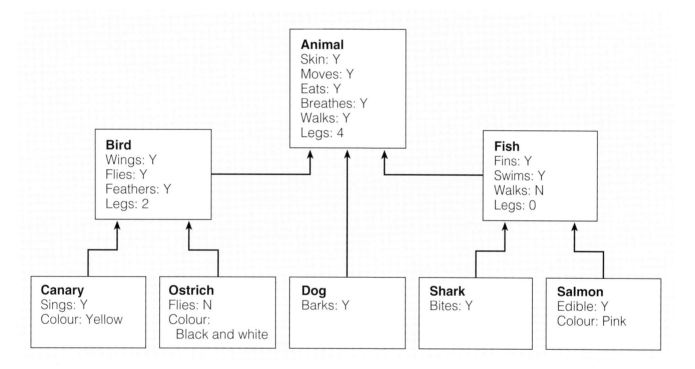

Figure 1.18   A frame network

In many frame systems, slots can have program fragments or function calls as fillers. This allows the frame system to do quite complex processing, while it remains, conceptually, a form of knowledge representation.

Scripts do much the same for processes and interactions. Given the story:

> Joe went to a restaurant. Joe ordered a hamburger. When the hamburger came, it was burnt to a crisp. Joe stormed out without paying.

we can be reasonably sure that Joe didn't eat the hamburger, even though that's not a fact that is explicitly mentioned in the story. We can do this because we seem to have a mental script of the events that take place during a visit to a restaurant, and we use this to fill in the unspoken details. Identifying such scripts allows systems to behave very flexibly, as every detail of every situation does not have to be spelt out every time.

A script is made up from a series of events, with each event expressed in **conceptual primitives**, such as moving from one place to another, building new information from old, or ingesting some substance. Having the complete script makes it easy for a system to make sense of a fragmentary narrative, as well as noticing strange or unusual events, such as food being overcooked. In a much-cited example, the SAM program, developed by Schank and Abelson, was provided with the story above and was also able to infer that Joe hadn't eaten the hamburger.

Other representations

You've already met various other representations. Production rules, which appeared in Section 7.2, are widely used. You have also developed a few representations yourself in some of the exercises. Throughout Symbolic AI, representations proliferate. Most of them are built for the specific task they are to support, but generally they can all be expressed (at least in principle) in the language of predicate logic, so that the limits on their use can be examined.

Exercise 1.21

Given the following tasks, which representations do you think would be the most suitable for each? You should use the criteria given in Section 8.2.

▶ theorem prover (a system that proves statements in mathematics and logic)

▶ expert system

▶ robotic arm control system

▶ speech-understanding system

▶ route-planning system.

The representations you have met include:

▶ propositional logic

▶ predicate logic

▶ frames

▶ scripts

▶ production rules

▶ some other, problem-specific representation.

Discussion ....

▶ *Theorem prover.* While these systems prove theorems (which are best represented as propositional or predicate logic formulae), the rules of inference used to generate the proofs, and the meta-knowledge needed to find those proofs, can be expressed in almost anything. As this is a deduction system, something like production rules might be suitable.

▶ *Expert system.* As we've seen above, production rules are very suitable for this application. The addition of some logical or mathematical ability could be useful if we were to include factors such as likelihood into an expert system.

▶ *Robotic arm control system.* Controlling a robotic arm involves two related problems. One is the issue of making the arm behave as the controller intends: this is a real-time control issue that involves lots of mathematics, but doesn't really count as AI. The other problem involves deciding what the arm should do to achieve its tasks. This planner needs to interface with the controller, and it needs to express the arm's goals and actions. A logic-based representation, similar to that given for chess, would seem to be the most suitable choice.

▶ *Speech-understanding system.* As with the robot arm, some low-level signal processing is needed to try to identify the sounds being produced. At this level, a logic-based representation seems to be the most appropriate. However, most of the intelligence in speech recognition systems comes from using what is already known to predict what's coming next. For this application, script-like representations could be useful.

▶ *Route-planning system.* The key elements here are towns, the routes between them and the lengths of those routes. As there is nothing requiring more complexity in the representation, a simple logic-based representation should suffice.

9 Reasoning

The physical symbol hypothesis, discussed in Section 4, proposes that all intelligent systems represent the world as a set of physical symbol expressions and reason by manipulating those expressions. I have spent much of this unit looking at different types of representations, along with their advantages and disadvantages. Now is the time to tackle the question of *reasoning* in such systems; in Unit 2 I will cover in detail the most widely used generic reasoning approach: heuristic search.

As you learned in Section 5, reasoning consists of manipulating a representation to achieve a goal state. The objective may be either the simple knowledge that the goal is achievable or, more often, the steps taken to transform the initial state into the goal.

At this point, it is worth pointing out the different criteria that the goal may have to fulfil. In some situations, such as the water jugs problem, there is a single goal state that must be achieved. In others, such as chess, the goal could be any one of a huge number of states (any of the positions of checkmate) – the task is simply to find one of them. Finally, as in our car-diagnostic example, there are many states that might satisfy us, but we want to find one that is somehow better than the others. As well as finding an adequate goal, we may also be concerned about the 'cost' of the path taken to find it. For some problems, we are not concerned with the number of steps needed to transform the initial state into the goal. For most problems, though, we may want to keep the number down to a minimum. If any valid solution is as good as any other, we term the problem a *satisfaction* problem. If the objective is not to find any solution, but to find a good (or even the best) solution, we term the problem an *optimisation* problem. You will recall that you first met the idea of an optimisation problem in Block 1, where I presented that old favourite, the Travelling Salesman Problem (TSP). Countless problems tackled in AI are optimisation problems of one form or another. I will return to them in Block 3.

SAQ 1.12

What is the difference between a satisfaction problem and an optimisation problem?

ANSWER..

A satisfaction problem is one in which any valid solution is as good as any other; an optimisation problem, by contrast, is one in which the objective is to find a good (or even) the best solution.

Recall from Section 5 that the physical symbol system hypothesis compels us to think of problems as being a set of discrete states (the state space), with operations on the state providing a means of moving from one state to another. Figure 1.19 shows an example state space for the water jugs problem. Starting at some initial state the reasoning process moves through the problem's state space, looking for a goal state. But, as we move through the search space, we have a limited horizon – we can only perceive the states that are neighbours of the one we are currently in. This means that we have to *search* through the state space until we find a goal state.

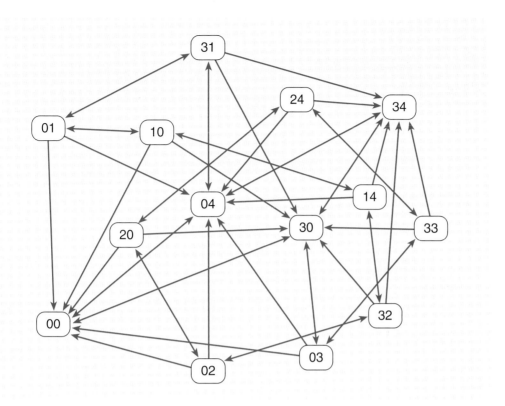

Figure 1.19   The state space of the water jugs problem. The numbers in each node are the amount of water in the three- and four-litre jugs, respectively

In this section, I will look at some general ways of enabling this vision of problem solving: forward and backward chaining, together with some ideas on how reasoning can be guided. In the next unit, I will look at specific techniques for search in more detail.

9.1 Forward and backward chaining

Reasoning is generally about trying to transform some initial state into a goal state by executing a series of processes that change the state. As you have just learned, we do this by searching the state space for a route from the initial state to the goal state, starting from our initial state and working towards the goal. This kind of reasoning is known as *forward chaining*. However, for some problems, we may find it more convenient to start with the desired goal state and try to find a path back to our initial state. In other cases, as I mentioned in Section 7.2, we might combine both methods. Backward chaining is useful if we have a clear idea of what the goal should be, but it is less so when we would be satisfied by any one of a number of possible goal states (such as any of the checkmate positions in chess). We can demonstrate each kind of reasoning using our expert system example, which clearly shows the difference in these approaches.

When an expert system does **forward chaining**, the system is primed with (or swiftly finds) a set of initial facts. If any subset of these facts match the premise of a rule (the If part), that rule is *fired* and its conclusions are added to the working knowledge. Reasoning finishes when an interesting conclusion is found or there are no more applicable rules to fire. Conversely, in **backward chaining**, the expert system is primed with a goal, a conclusion that it wants to prove or disprove. The system then searches through the knowledge base to find some combination of rules that lead to that conclusion. The premises of those rules then become subgoals and the expert system tries to prove them in turn, perhaps by using other rules or by asking the user questions.

To illustrate, let's use the rules given in Box 1.4, part of an expert system that diagnoses the fault in a car that doesn't start. The ASKABLE clause lists the facts that the system can ask the user questions about (other facts the system has to infer for itself). The CONCLUSIONS clause lists the conclusions that the expert system can find: as soon as one of these conclusions appears in working memory, the expert system knows it has found the fault and can stop the consultation.

Box 1.4: A sample set of rules for a car diagnosis expert system

```
RULE 1:
IF NOT engine-turns-over
    AND NOT headlights-are-bright
THEN problem-with-battery

RULE 2:
IF engine-getting-petrol
    AND engine-turns-over
    AND NOT smell-of-petrol
THEN problem-with-spark-plugs

RULE 3:
IF NOT engine-turns-over
    AND headlights-are-bright
THEN problem-with-starter-motor

RULE 4:
IF engine-turns-over
    AND smell-of-petrol
    AND engine-getting-petrol
THEN problem-engine-flooded

RULE 5:
IF petrol-in-fuel-tank
THEN engine-getting-petrol

ASKABLE: engine-turns-over, petrol-in-fuel-tank,
headlights-are-bright, smell-of-petrol

CONCLUSIONS: problem-engine-flooded, problem-with-battery,
problem-with-spark-plugs, problem-with-starter-motor
```

Let's start by looking at how forward chaining works to find the fault. The process operates as a two-stage cycle:

1   The system checks all the rules against the working memory and finds those that have true antecedents but have not yet fired.

2   The system chooses one of these rules and adds its consequent as a new fact to the working memory.

The process then returns to the first stage, fires another rule that now has true antecedents, and so on until a conclusion is found or there are no more rules to be fired. When an expert system has not reached a conclusion, it will ask the user for more information, which may enable it to derive more knowledge and then a conclusion.

These choices are termed *conflicts* and choosing between them is termed *conflict resolution*.

At either of the above stages, the inference engine may be faced with choices. There will often be several rules that could fire, based on the current state of the working knowledge; the order in which to fire them has to be decided. Similarly, there may be a number of questions that could be put to the user, and the inference engine will have to choose which to ask. How these conflicts are resolved depends on the kind of meta-knowledge the system has been supplied with. In this example, I'll use the very simple conflict resolution strategy of always choosing the first applicable option.

Box 1.5 shows a sample consultation using the rule set in Box 1.4 and demonstrates how forward chaining works in practice:

1   The expert system initially knows nothing about the situation. This means that none of the rules can fire, so it quickly moves on to asking a question of the user. It looks at the ASKABLE list and poses the first unasked question there – whether the engine turns over perhaps in the form 'Is it true: engine-turns-over?'). The answer 'yes' is lodged in working memory.

2   The system returns to the rule-firing stage. At this stage, none of the rules can fire so the inference engine looks for another askable fact, this time about the fuel tank.

3   After this question is answered positively, the system returns to rule firing and finds that Rule 5 can fire. As this is the only such rule, there is no conflict, and so the fact engine-getting-petrol is added to working memory.

4   Once this fact is added, no more rules can fire so the system asks the next question.

5   No more rules fire until after the last question is asked, when Rule 2 fires. This adds the fact problem-with-spark-plugs to working memory. As this fact is marked as a conclusion, the consultation stops and the expert system states this result.

Box 1.5: A sample consultation with a forward-chaining expert system

```
Is it true: engine-turns-over?
> Y
Is it true: petrol-in-fuel-tank?
> Y
Is it true: headlights-are-bright?
> Y
Is it true: smell-of-petrol?
> N
Conclusion: problem-with-spark-plugs
```

Exercise 1.22

Consider this consultation:

```
Is it true: engine-turns-over?
> N
Is it true: petrol-in-fuel-tank?
> Y
Is it true: headlights-are-bright?
> N
Conclusion: problem-with-battery
```

Describe what the expert system is doing at each stage in this consultation.

Discussion ....

The first question concerns the first askable fact. The answer 'no' is lodged in working memory. No rules can fire with this fact, so a question about the next askable fact is posed. The answer 'yes' is recorded and Rule 5 fired, adding the fact 'engine-getting-petrol' to the working memory. No more rules can fire so a question about the next askable fact is asked. The negative answer about bright headlights means that Rule 1 is fired and generates the conclusion.

Let's now look at how backward chaining works using the sample consultation in Box 1.6.

Box 1.6: A sample consultation with a backward-chaining expert system

```
Is it true: engine-turns-over?
> Y
Is it true: smell-of-petrol?
> N
Is it true: petrol-in-fuel-tank?
> Y
Conclusion: problem-with-spark-plugs
```

Recall that backward chaining starts by the system choosing (or being given) a conclusion to prove (which I'll call the hypothesis) and then working backwards through the rules to find the questions it has to ask in order to prove or disprove that hypothesis. For instance, using the rule set above, the expert system will work through the conclusions list, taking each in turn as a hypothesis, until it is able to prove one of them. Let's say it starts by trying to prove that the problem with the car is that the engine is flooded. The process proceeds as follows:

1   It finds all the rules that have engine-is-flooded as a consequent (in this case, only Rule 4). The expert system then chooses one of these rules and attempts to prove that its antecedent is true.

2   The antecedent of Rule 4 is a conjunction of three terms, so the expert system must prove all of these terms to allow it to draw the conclusion engine-is-flooded. The first conjunct, engine-turns-over, is not the consequent of any rule but is marked as askable, so the expert system asks the user this question.

3   The answer 'yes' is consistent with the hypothesis, so the system asks about the second part of Rule 4's antecedent. The answer 'no' means that Rule 4's antecedent cannot be true.

4   As there are no other rules that would allow the expert system to prove the conclusion engine-is-flooded, it abandons this hypothesis.

5   The next hypothesis it considers, problem-with-battery, also cannot be true because the only rule that could conclude cannot fire because the system knows the engine turns over.

6   The system then moves on to consider the third possible conclusion, problem-with-spark-plugs. Rule 2 is applicable here and the expert system tries to prove its antecedent.

7   The first part of Rule 2's antecedent, engine-getting-petrol, is itself the consequent of another rule, Rule 5. So, to prove problem-with-spark plugs, the system has to prove Rule 2 is true.

8   To prove Rule 2 is true, it has to prove Rule 5 is true. To prove Rule 5, it has to ask the user. This gives rise to the last question in Box 1.5. The answer allows the expert system to add engine-getting-petrol to the working memory.

9   The remaining parts of Rule 2's antecedent can be found from looking in working memory, so the expert system can deduce that its hypothesis, problem-with-spark-plugs, is correct.

Generally, a real expert system uses a combination of forward and backward chaining. It may use forward chaining initially to discover some basic facts and use them to propose a possible solution it will try to prove or disprove. It then changes to backward chaining focused on that proposal until it is either proved or disproved. If it is disproved, it may then revert to forward chaining to find another hypothesis. If the proposal is proven, the system may then forward chain from the conclusion (such as the diagnosis of a fault in a car) to suggest actions to take. The control of such changes in reasoning strategy, as well as deciding which of several possible rules to use next, is determined by the system's meta-knowledge, knowledge about its own knowledge. Differences in meta-knowledge can have a profound effect on the system's performance. This topic is discussed briefly in the next section.

Exercise 1.23

Consider the following problems:

▶ game playing

▶ car diagnosis

▶ organising a holiday.

In each case, is the problem best solved using forward chaining, backward chaining or a combination of the two? Briefly explain your reasoning.

Discussion ....

▶ Game playing: probably best solved by forward chaining. Many games have a large number of winning or losing positions. Trying to pick the one that will be achieved, in order to reason from it to the current position, is unlikely to be feasible. It's better to reason from the single, given position and see where a sequence of moves takes you.

▶ Car diagnosis: as I've discussed above, a combination of forward and backward chaining is probably the best approach. Initial forward chaining can be used to get a handle on the problem. This should suggest a possible diagnosis, and backward chaining can then be used to confirm or deny it.

▶ Organising a holiday: backwards chaining would seem to be the way to go here. The requirements of what needs organising are easy to specify in advance. Once the requirements are there, you can reason backwards from them to the actions that are needed to ensure that they are fulfilled.

9.2 Guiding reasoning

In Section 8.1 I pointed out that knowledge comes in different forms, which are used differently in reasoning. The main distinction I want to concentrate on here is the one between base-level knowledge (knowledge about a domain) and meta-knowledge (knowledge about knowledge). Base-level knowledge is used in reasoning about the processes that are possible in a domain, such as the moves allowed in chess. Meta-knowledge may include factors such as the costs or benefits of an action, which make it possible for a problem-solving system to select between the choices available to it. It is here that much of the intelligence of the system lies.

One simple and powerful way of representing such meta-knowledge is to measure the 'goodness' of each state. Even if a particular state is not a goal state, we can often produce some measure of its closeness to the goal. We can imagine this as being the 'height' of a state, and therefore imagine a 'landscape' over which we search, with the better states forming hills and the worse states forming valleys. We can use this information to guide the search for a goal, and the measure of how this is done is covered in detail in the next unit. If we are searching for a single goal state, we think of searching for the highest peak in that landscape. If we are faced with a problem where any satisfying solution would do, we can imagine a 'snow line' that divides satisfactory solutions from the low-lying unsatisfactory ones (see Figure 1.20).

Figure 1.20   The idea of a 'snow line' on mountain peaks

By exploiting well-founded strategies, known as **heuristics**, the system can focus its reasoning on the parts of the problem space that are likely to be fruitful. By avoiding parts of the search space that will not lead to a satisfactory solution, the system can avoid the expensive exploration of those areas and its attention can be directed to those avenues that will lead to the goal. The next unit will examine one approach to implementing this idea.

SAQ 1.13

What advantages come from using meta-knowledge to guide the reasoning process?

ANSWER...

Efficiency. While this may not sound like a compelling reason, it almost always makes the difference between a process that is too slow to produce any solution and one that *may* work in practice. All the interesting AI problems are too complex to solve by brute-force methods, and the intelligence to solve them cleverly normally resides in meta-knowledge.

10 Summary of Unit 1

This unit has covered the basic groundwork of Symbolic AI and discussed one of its pillars, representation. It introduced the notion of the physical symbol system hypothesis (PSSH) as the starting point of Symbolic AI: the hypothesis that all intelligent thought is symbolic manipulation. From this, I considered how to represent problems and what makes a good representation. I then looked briefly at reasoning and the concepts of meta-knowledge and meta-reasoning.

I proposed that reasoning in Symbolic AI can be seen in terms of a state-space representation and finding a way of transforming an initial state into a desired state. The next unit will take this idea and explore it in greater depth as it considers the idea of search as a problem-solving method.

Now look back at the learning outcomes for this unit and check these against what you think you can now do. Return to any section of the unit if you need to.

Unit 2: Search

CONTENTS

Introduction to Unit 2

In Unit 1 I introduced the physical symbol system hypothesis (PSSH), which in a nutshell states that a physical system (or a problem) can be represented by symbols and reasoning can be made through manipulation of these symbols. I looked at a number of representation examples. You have also learnt about the separate roles of representation and reasoning in Symbolic AI.

In this unit, I look at how search techniques can be employed to reason. I start by defining what search is and look at some daily activities that require search. With the aid of two classical problems (the route-planning and missionaries-and-cannibals problems), I look at how search can be used to solve these and many other problems. Search comes in two main types: uninformed (also called blind) search, and informed (also called heuristic) search. Blind search goes through all possible solutions until it finds the goal. Although not efficient, it's easy to understand. We can use it to illustrate the operation principle of searches. Informed search is more efficient. It uses knowledge to guide the search so that it can usually find a solution more quickly. Finally, I look at how search techniques can be applied in other areas, such as game playing.

What you need to study this unit

You will need the following course components, and will need to use your computer and internet connection for some of the exercises.

▶ this Block 2 text

▶ the course DVD.

LEARNING OUTCOMES FOR UNIT 2

After studying this unit you will be able to:

2.1 understand the role of search in Symbolic AI;

2.2 employ the terminology related to search techniques;

2.3 describe how various uninformed and informed search algorithms operate;

2.4 compare and contrast uninformed and informed searches;

2.5 describe the minimax algorithm for adversarial search;

2.6 apply the minimax algorithm with α-β pruning to a sample game tree.

2 The need for search

These days, when the term 'search' is used in a computer context, it is usually taken to mean exploration of the World Wide Web for documents, an activity carried out by Google and other search engines. However, the form of search I'm going to discuss in this unit is quite different in purpose and in kind from an internet search. It is a hugely important topic not just in Symbolic AI, but in the field of AI generally.

You will already know from your reading of Block 1 and of Unit 1 of this block that search has been seen as playing a key role in Symbolic AI since its earliest days. The AI pioneers of the 1940s and 1950s identified the operation of an intelligent computer system as being a search through representations of the states of a complex problem. They believed that search techniques could be applied in this way to more or less any problem that required an intelligent solution. Before I discuss the terminology of search and how it can be achieved, let's consider some everyday activities.

Exercise 2.1

Think about some of your daily problems or activities. To what extent could any of these be expressed as a search problem?

Discussion ....

I thought of a few, as follows:

▶ I recently lost my car keys (problem) – I frequently do. I tried to find them (solution) by searching the places I had visited recently.

▶ I planned a trip to Lancashire (problem), which required me to search maps for a suitable route and schedule an itinerary for when I got there (solution).

▶ It brings me joy to thrash my next door neighbour at chess, so I am always trying to find the best possible move against him (problem) by searching and evaluating each possible move (solution).

▶ At weekends, I try to plan my work for the week ahead (seldom very successfully). This involves finding the best sequence of tasks and the days and times on which to carry them out (problem); to find such a sequence, I generally have to search through a whole set of possible schemes by trial and error until I arrive at the one that seems best (solution).

In Unit 1, I identified some of the common characteristics of such search activities:

▶ goals, such as to locate my keys, to find the best route, to decide the best move in a chess game, and so on;

▶ a particular point at which they start: the point where I first noticed my keys were lost, a particular board position, a blank sheet of paper for my plan or itinerary;

▶ many possible paths along which to search: for instance, the lost key might have been mislaid at any of the places that I'd last visited, or the places before that, or the places before that;

▶ factors determining which search paths I can take that may depend on where I am, and where I've searched already. To take a simple example, if – in building up my Lancashire itinerary – I've already included a visit to the British Lawnmower Museum ('A glimpse into the fascinating world of garden machinery') in Southport, I probably wouldn't want to include it again. One visit would surely be enough.

There are other characteristics of search that I'll look at in a moment. However, to bring together some of the points I made in Unit 1 of this block, we can characterise the kind of search that takes place in Symbolic AI systems as follows:

▶ It is a process of attempting to find a *goal state* from the *initial state*.

▶ For complex problems, the search usually needs to go through a large number of *intermediate states* before it reaches the goal state.

▶ The set of all possible states form the **state space**, also called the **search space** or **problem space**.

▶ To progress from one state to another state, *operators* are required. An operator describes what actions are executed to change the state.

This is the basic pattern I established in Unit 1: initial state, goal state, state space and operator. But there are certain comments we can make on it:

▶ There are often a number of possible operators that can be applied to any one state, but sometimes a particular operator may not be applicable in certain states. There are cases in which it is forbidden to move to some states, as these are illegal. For example, if it is my turn to move in chess, it's not possible to select any operator that will take me to a position in which I am in check.

▶ The goal state may not be reachable because the time or effort required is too great, such as searching through all possible chess positions before I die of old age.

▶ The goal state may not be reachable at all. For example, it simply might not be possible to get to a particularly fine viewing point on the Lancashire coast because no roads or paths go there.

▶ The task may not be just to search for a solution, but to find the best solution among several possibilities, a point I made in Block 1.

In summary, then, search is a process of stepping through points (states) in a state space towards a goal state, often with constraints on which states can be visited. Let me try to set up the discussion of the rest of the unit by putting all the above points into context. Let's revisit two familiar Symbolic AI problems, ones that you've met earlier in the course: route planning and missionaries and cannibals.

Example 1 – Route planning

Let's start with quite a simple problem, which I presented earlier in Unit 1. The task is for a computer system to plan a route from Exeter to Leeds by road. Obviously the sort of information we need – places and routes – is represented by road maps, and these would be our first port of call. Figure 2.1 shows a large-scale map of England, representing the locations of Exeter, Bristol, Manchester, Leeds and London, and the motorways and other roads linking these cities. However, this sort of information is highly visual and could not be processed directly by a computer. As I made clear in Unit 1, we will need to find a form of *representation* for the information. The table I showed you there probably wouldn't be sufficient for this purpose; we would most likely have to use some purely symbolic form, perhaps something like this:

roadBetween(*Exeter*,*Bristol*,74)

roadBetween(*Exeter*,*Manchester*,236)

roadBetween(*Exeter*,*Leeds*,278)

roadBetween(*Bristol*,*Manchester*,165)

roadBetween(*Bristol*,*Leeds*,207)

...

and so on. Note that I've simplified the problem down to its bare bones, just for the sake of this discussion. In reality, as you can see from Figure 2.1, there will be many roads between the various cities, and thus a much greater complexity of possible routes.

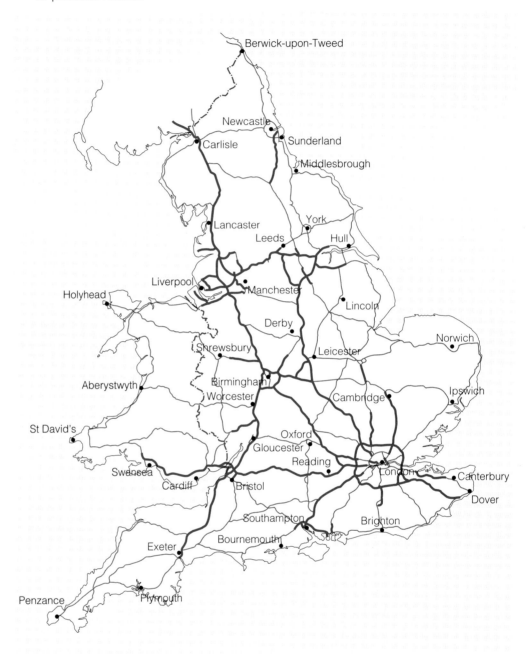

Figure 2.1   Conventional road map

Example 2 – Missionaries and cannibals

I also introduced the missionaries and cannibals in Unit 1. To save you having to look back at it, it can be briefly restated here. Three missionaries and three cannibals are to cross a river using a boat. However, the boat can only take one or two people at a time. To prevent their being eaten, the missionaries must never be outnumbered by the cannibals at anytime or anywhere.

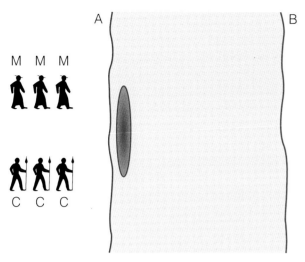

Figure 2.2   Missionaries-and-cannibals problem

It's easy to come up with witty pictorial representations of the information we need, such as in Figure 2.2. However, these are not likely to be of any use to a computer either. Again, we need a purely symbolic, bare representation of all the relevant facts needed for a solution, leaving out all the irrelevant ones. One way to represent the problem symbolically is to denote the opposite banks of the river as A and B, a missionary by m, a cannibal by c and the boat by b. Then the state pictured in Figure 2.2 could be represented by the two expressions:

bankA(mmm,ccc,b)

bankB()

or something similar.

Now let's review the points I made above about search, in the context of these two problems.

2.1   States and operators

We can dispense with these two topics in the following easy question.

SAQ 2.1

Note down the start state, goal state and operators of both the route-planning and the missionaries-and-cannibals problems.

ANSWER..

The initial state of the route-planning problem is Exeter, the departure point of the route. The goal state is obviously Leeds, the destination. From Exeter (the initial state) to Leeds (the goal state), the route may pass through numerous other places, each one an intermediate state. An operator is any move that moves from the current city to a new city.

In the missionaries-and-cannibals problem, a state is any disposition of missionaries, cannibals and boat across the two banks. The initial state, for instance, is the one pictured in Figure 2.2, with all three missionaries, all three cannibals and the boat at river bank A. The goal state is all three missionaries and all three cannibals (and the boat) at river bank B. An operator changes the personnel on each bank and the position of the boat.

Simple. But not completely simple. There are one or two complications. In the route-planning problem, note that although there is a route from Exeter to Leeds that bypasses all other towns, other routes to Leeds via intermediate destinations are not precluded. For certain starting points, there may be no direct road. In other cases the route via intermediate towns might be better. But what do we mean by 'better' here? Shortest? Smallest estimated travelling time? Most scenic? Obviously, it all depends on what we're trying to do. There has to be some objective criterion according to which we can evaluate how good each possible route is. Any of the criteria I suggested above would do (although one would have to specify some objective way of evaluating the scenic properties of a route). In the field of AI, we use the term **fitness** to describe how good a solution is. The solution with highest fitness will be the best. In the route-planning problem, the purpose of the search may very well be not just to find a route (obviously there are many), but to find the solution with the maximum fitness. In other words, it's an *optimisation problem*. However, remember that a good solution doesn't imply a perfect solution. For many real-world problems, it may be very difficult to find the best possible solution within realistic time and memory limits. I'll come back to this point later. Apart from fitness, we may also need to consider the **cost** of finding a solution, in terms of the time and/or memory requirements of finding a solution. Ideally, we would want to minimise the cost of the search as well as maximising the fitness of the solution.

Optimisation problems were introduced in Block 1

Defining the operators in the route-planning problem is not entirely straightforward either. Operators just move the system from one state to another state, so many possible operators could be defined here, depending on what it is one wants the system to do. While navigating with a GPS system, for instance, we might have three basic operators – namely go straight (for a particular distance), turn left (by a certain number of degrees) and turn right (by a certain number of degrees). However, for planning a route for long-distance driving, we probably wouldn't need such detailed instructions: it might be more appropriate to define operators such as keep on this road, take the exit at the next junction or at so-and-so junction number, join a particular road, etc. Again, if one is only interested in the order of cities to visit, operators to move from one city to another would be appropriate.

The missionaries-and-cannibals problem presents rather different complications. In contrast to our route-planning example, where every state is connected to every other state, certain states in the former problem are unreachable from others. For example in state:

bankA(m,c,b)

bankB($mm,cc,\_$)

one simply can't move to:

bankA(mm,cc,b)

bankB($m,c,\_$)

as the rules don't allow it.

SAQ 2.2

Why is this move not allowed?

ANSWER...

The move involves one missionary and one cannibal moving from bank B to bank A, but the boat starts on bank A.

Only a subset of operators are generally allowed in any one state. Moreover, there are states to which we could move theoretically, but which are illegal. For example, in state:

bankA(mmm,ccc,b)

bankB(_,_,_)

there is an operator available to move to:

bankA(m,ccc,_)

bankB(mm,_,b)

but this would be forbidden, as the resulting state means that the cannibals on bank A will instantly gang up on the lone missionary there.

Note also that the purposes of the search are different in missionaries and cannibals. The problem does have several solutions, some of them convoluted, but there is no particular cost associated with the idea of travelling from one bank to the other. One is not necessarily looking for any best solution, merely a legal solution. In defining the operators, too, there is no real problem about the level of detail at which they should be specified. An operator straightforwardly moves one or more figures and the boat to the other bank.

2.2 | State spaces

I touched on the idea of a state space in Unit 1 of this block and earlier in this unit. Basically, the state space of a particular problem will be a set whose elements comprise the start state, the goal state and all possible intermediate states. Furthermore, if we are representing the space pictorially, we can show the legal transitions between these states as lines connecting these states. So a possible representation of the state space for the route-planning problem might look like Figure 2.3.

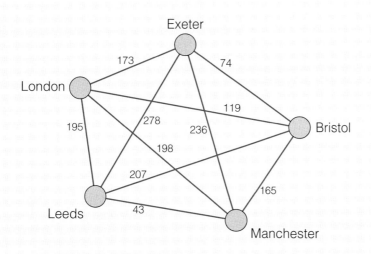

Figure 2.3   State space for route-planning problem

Note that I've included the distances, which may contribute to the fitness of a possible solution. This kind of figure is known as a **cyclic graph**, as it contains backward loops. One could draw a similar diagram of the state space of the missionaries-and-cannibals problem, although here the state space is bigger, so to represent all of it would mean a more complicated graph.

Exercise 2.2

On a bit of scrap paper, have a go at picturing the state space for the missionaries-and-cannibals problem. You can use a simplified form of representation of each state like {mm,cc,b}, {m,c,_}, where the contents of the first set of brackets represent the personnel on bank A and the second those on bank B. Don't try to represent the whole space: just sketch a few states, to give the general idea.

Discussion ....

As the boat can only take one or two people at a time and the journeys are directional, there are ten possible operators:

1   The boat carries one missionary (m) from bank A to B.

2   The boat carries two missionaries (m,m) from bank A to B.

3   The boat carries one cannibal (c) from bank A to B.

4   The boat carries two cannibals (c,c) from bank A to B.

5   The boat carries one missionary and one cannibal (m,c) from bank A to B.

6   The boat carries one missionary (m) from bank B to A.

7   The boat carries two missionaries (m,m) from bank B to A.

8   The boat carries one cannibal (c) from bank B to A.

9   The boat carries two cannibals (c,c) from bank B to A.

10 The boat carries one missionary and one cannibal (m,c) from bank B to A.

So, after some fiddling about, I arrived at the depiction in Figure 2.4.

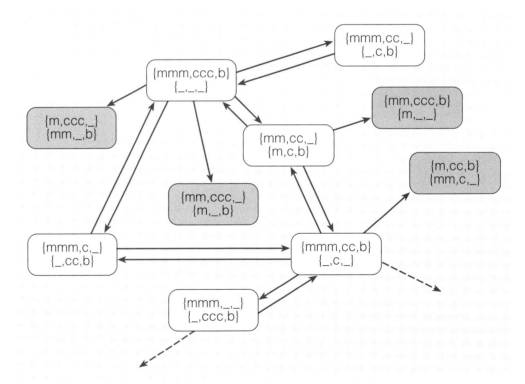

Figure 2.4   Part of the state space for the missionaries-and-cannibals problem

Note that this is only *part* of the state space. I marked illegal states as shaded; and, although there might theoretically be moves out of illegal states, I've not shown these, as illegal states are never entered. You can also see that there are numerous dead ends.

You are probably already objecting that the cycles in both state spaces are an unnecessary distraction. After all, having moved from Exeter to Manchester, say, we are hardly likely to want to go straight back to Exeter again. In fact it's unlikely that we would want to revisit Exeter at all, except in very special circumstances. And if you look closely at Figure 2.3 you can see that – as well as the possibility of simply going Exeter → Manchester → Exeter – there are any number of more roundabout ways of going back to the start state. The same is true in missionaries and cannibals. Our common sense tells us that, if you want to make progress, you don't generally go straight back to where you came from. But computers have no common sense. If an operator is available to move straight back to the previous state, there is no special reason why a computer search process might not select it. What we have to do is specify the rules of search in such a way that prevents the system from making such a choice, or ever revisiting a state that it has already been in. If we do this then the cyclic graphs of Figures 2.3 and 2.4 become a kind of **acyclic graph** familiar to computer scientists as a **tree**, as in Figure 2.5.

Actually, this example is a directed acyclic graph, but the principle holds.

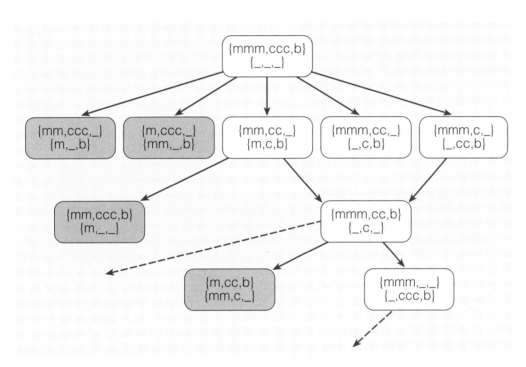

Figure 2.5   Part of the revised state space for the missionaries-and-cannibals problem (cycles excluded)

2.3   Search

So, in cases such as our two examples, a search of the state space is an exploration of a tree of possibilities. The aim is to find a path from the root of the tree (the start state) through to some leaf node that represents a goal state, as illustrated in Figure 2.6. The solution will be the sequence of nodes that were visited. In the case of the missionaries-and-cannibals problem, there are various solutions. My attempt is shown in Table 2.1. The numbers of the operators I used are given in the discussion section of Exercise 2.2 above.

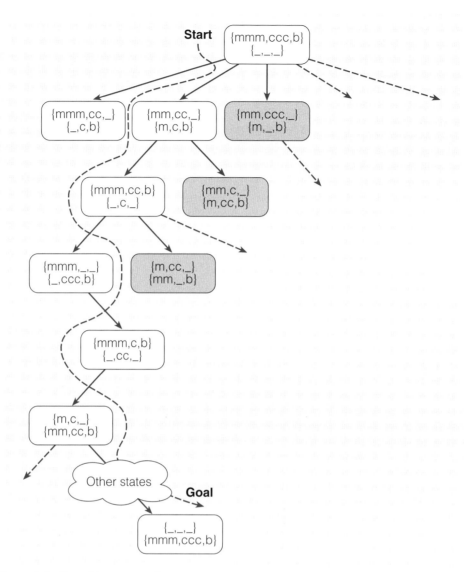

Figure 2.6   Searching a tree of states

Table 2.1 My attempt at solving the missionaries-and-cannibals problem

State	Operator	Bank A	Bank B	Remark
0		{mmm,ccc,b}	{_,_,_}	Initial state
1	5	{mm,cc,_}	{m,c,b}	One missionary and one cannibal moved from A to B
2	6	{mmm,cc,b}	{_,c,_}	One missionary moved from B to A
3	4	{mmm,_,_}	{_,ccc,b}	Two cannibals moved from A to B
4	8	{mmm,c,b}	{_,cc,_}	One cannibal moved from B to A
5	2	{m,c,_}	{mm,cc,b}	Two missionaries moved from A to B
6	10	{mm,cc,b}	{m,c,_}	One missionary and one cannibal moved from B to A
7	2	{_,cc,_}	{mmm,c,b}	Two missionaries moved from A to B
8	8	{_,ccc,b}	{mmm,_,_}	One cannibal moved from B to A
9	4	{_,c,_}	{mmm,cc,b}	Two cannibals moved from A to B
10	8	{_,cc,b}	{mmm,c,_}	One cannibal moved from B to A
11	4	{_,_,_}	{mmm,ccc,b}	Two cannibals moved from A to B (Goal state reached)

This all looks fairly straightforward. However, I do want to emphasise at this point just how much intelligence and common sense we humans bring to even quite simple problems like these, usually without really noticing it. For a start, visual representations give us many clues – just look at the map in Figure 2.1. In building up the sequence of moves, we remember the states we've already visited; we know not to do stupid things like go back to where we've just come from; we form estimates of what might be the best path to take next; we use common sense and specialised knowledge; we look ahead. Few of these resources are available to a computer. The best metaphor with which to visualise a computer search of a state space would be that of a person creeping around a maze, with no memory of where he has been, no power to see the overall pattern of the maze from above, forced at each junction to make a choice between a number of identical-seeming alternative paths.

SAQ 2.3

How do you think the furniture-moving activity I discussed in Unit 1 of this block might utilise search techniques? Identify the initial and goal states and define some example operators. Can you also suggest ways of determining the fitness and cost?

ANSWER...

The goal is that the furniture is placed in different locations that are pleasing to the eye and convenient to the user. The initial state is the pieces of furniture in their initial positions before they are moved. For this example, several operators would be required. Some possible operators are: moving a table from location A to B, moving a chair from location C to D, moving a bookshelf from location X to Y etc.

The goal can be subjective, so a suitable set of fitness criteria would have to specified, to test that the goal had been reached. One example criterion might be that the amount of free space in the centre of the room is maximised. The cost can be determined by the total number of times furniture would have to be moved, or the time required to find an acceptable layout.

Now that we have developed some terminology – states, goal, state space, operators, fitness and cost – with which to talk about search, we can move on to discuss how search by computer can be conducted. You may remember that I likened computer search of a state space to a person creeping around a maze, with no overall view and only able to make informed selections of which path to take whenever there is a choice. You may wonder how this can be done by a computer. What search strategies can be programmed into it? In the rest of the unit, I am going to look at two main categories of search, **uninformed search** and **informed search**. Within these two overarching classes, there are many different techniques available and I want to cover some of the most common ones.

As we explore the search algorithms, you need to keep in mind three desirable factors that we would like any search process to have. These are:

▶ **Completeness**. Does the search process find a route to the goal, if one exists?

▶ **Optimality**. Does the search find the best route to the goal?

▶ **Complexity**. Does the search process consume large amounts of either time or space (memory) in finding a solution?

As you will see, the development of search algorithms is an attempt to produce a search process that gives satisfactory answers to all three of these questions.

3 Uninformed search

This section and the next take a practical approach to understanding how these search algorithms operate. You will be using (and modifying) a piece of software called SearchLab to explore and understand search via a number of computer exercises. If, for whatever reason, you can't do the exercises while you're reading the text for the first time, you should come back to them later to consolidate your understanding of this topic.

We now have to develop an algorithm that will allow us to search a state space. The key to the algorithm is the **agenda**, a data structure that holds all the states that we want to explore in the order in which we want to explore them. The agenda initially contains just the starting state. We apply the operators to this state to generate new states, which are, in turn, placed on the agenda. This process is known as **expanding** that state. Then we continue to cycle through the agenda, taking the first state from the agenda, testing to see if it is a goal state, applying the operators and adding the expanded states to the agenda. As we often want to know how to go from the start state to the goal state, the agenda will contain **paths** from the start state to the current state. I've stated this algorithm more formally in Box 2.1.

Box 2.1: The generic search algorithm

```
find_path_to_goal (start_node, goal_test, operators)
   return search (enqueue (start_node, []), goal_test, operators)
end

search (agenda, goal_test, operators)
   if empty (agenda) then
      return with failure
   else
      set current_path (first agenda)
      set agenda (butfirst agenda)
      if goal (current_path)        ; success!
         return path
      else
         set successors (apply (operators, current_path))
         set agenda (enqueue (successors, agenda))
         return search (start_node, goal_test, operators)
      end
   end
end
```

Note that this is a *generic* algorithm, a basic pattern. Variations on how we find the successors of a state and how those successors are queued give rise to different search algorithms that behave in very different ways.

Uninformed search, as its name suggests, uses no information about the problem to guide the search. Instead, the agent simply moves blindly (though systematically) through the search space until it stumbles upon a goal state. This approach may not be efficient, but it is simple and so makes a good starting point for understanding search. As an example, I'll use the route-planning problem (see Figure 2.7), travelling from Exeter to Lincoln. In Figure 2.7, towns less than 140 miles by road are connected by links, showing that a person can travel directly from one to another.

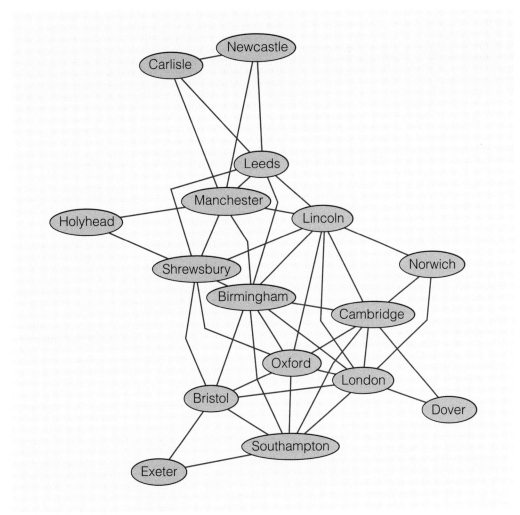

Figure 2.7   The state space for route planning

There are two basic uninformed search algorithms: **breadth-first search** and **depth-first search**. They differ only in how the successor states are added to the agenda.

Computer Exercise 2.1

Now find Computer Exercise 2.1 on the course DVD and follow the instructions. This exercise explores the differences between depth-first and breadth-first search.

The difference between the two strategies will become clearer when I look at the search tree explored by the two algorithms (see Figure 2.8). Both strategies examine nodes in the same search tree, but Boxes 2.2 and 2.3 show that this tree is explored in different ways. Essentially, the difference is in the *order* in which nodes are examined. Breadth-first search explores all the states at a given depth in the tree before moving on to the next layer, visiting the nodes in the order illustrated in Figure 2.8. In contrast, depth-first search always examines the children of the current node before examining any of its siblings at the same level. The depth-first strategy will explore the first child and all its descendents first and will only move its attention towards the other children if the first child leads to a dead end.

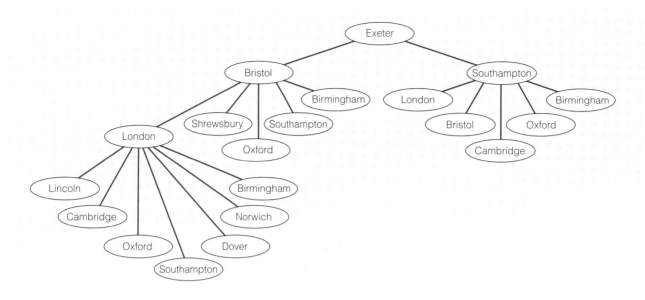

Figure 2.8   Search tree for going from Exeter to Lincoln

The difference between these two search algorithms lies simply in how the agenda is updated. With breadth-first search, the successors of a state are added to the end of the agenda; with depth-first search, the successors are added to the front of the agenda.

Computer Exercise 2.2

Now do Computer Exercise 2.2 on the course DVD, where you will use the SearchLab software to check for yourself that these two methods of updating the agenda result in the search strategies I've described. You may want to look at the reported agendas, generated by SearchLab, shown in Boxes 2.2 and 2.3.

Box 2.2: Nodes examined by breadth-first search

```
Examining exeter
Examining bristol
Examining southampton
Examining london
Examining shrewsbury
Examining oxford
Examining southampton
Examining birmingham
Examining london
Examining bristol
Examining cambridge
Examining oxford
Examining birmingham
Examining lincoln
Found route from exeter to lincoln : [exeter bristol london lincoln]
(331 miles) (14 nodes visited)
```

Box 2.3: Nodes examined by depth-first search

```
Examining exeter
Examining bristol
Examining london
Examining lincoln
Found route from exeter to lincoln : [exeter bristol london lincoln]
(331 miles) (4 nodes visited)
```

In this example, it would seem that depth-first search is the better approach: it finds the route from Exeter to Lincoln after examining fewer states than breadth-first search. However, that was chance in this case: compare the routes from Exeter to Cambridge found by depth-first and breadth-first search. Breadth-first search has the advantage that it will always find the route (if one exists) with the least number of intermediate states, but at the expense of having to keep on the agenda every path with this number of steps. This can be quite large: it will be about b^m or $5^3 = 125$ paths for the three-step path from Exeter to Lincoln, where m is the number of links in the path and b is the branching factor, the average number of children of each node of a graph. In this example, b is just over 5.

Depth-first search can be used to reduce the memory requirements of search. Depth-first search only explores one path at a time, such as the path shown in Figure 2.9. It doesn't need to know about the other possible paths until the one it is exploring turns out to be a dead end. It is only if Lincoln turns out to be a dead end that the search algorithm needs to know about the other neighbours of London in the search space.

In this case the search is said to **backtrack** from Lincoln to London and make another choice about the way to proceed from London. This means that we can limit the memory usage of depth-first search to being linear in the length of the path rather than exponential, as it is for breadth-first search. We can do this if we allow the states in our search tree to be more active participants in the process. Rather than generate all the successors of a node when that node is visited, we can replace the nodes with structures resembling Java collections with iterators. When a node is first visited, it states its first successor, but the node object will not generate the next successor until it is requested by the search process. This way of implementing search doesn't require an agenda at all, as the search tree is kept implicit in the states of the objects representing the nodes visited. However, since this approach is implemented very differently from other search algorithms, I won't look at it again here.

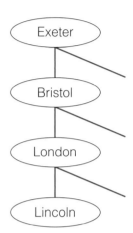

Figure 2.9   The minimal search tree needed by depth-first search

You can see backtracking occur when SearchLab looks for a route from Exeter to Norwich. When the search visits Shrewsbury, it first tries Holyhead, realises that this is a dead-end (Manchester having already been visited), backtracks to Shrewsbury and then tries the route to Oxford.

Exercise 2.3

How do depth-first and breadth-first searches fulfil the criteria of completeness, optimality and complexity?

Discussion ....

Breadth-first search is complete (it will always find a solution if one exists), so long as the search space is **locally finite** (i.e. no state has an infinite number of successors). It will find the solution with the smallest number of steps, but this is not necessarily the shortest route, so it isn't optimal. It uses a lot of space for the agenda, so its space complexity is high

Depth-first search, when applied to a finite tree, is complete. However, if the search space is infinite – as it is for search on graphs without cycle checking – depth-first search may start off down one avenue that will not lead to the goal, and never reach a point where it is forced to backtrack. Even if that is not the case, it may find a very roundabout route, so it is by no means optimal. Using the representation above, it's very efficient in terms of space (only the current path needs to be stored) but is complex in terms of time, because of backtracking and the exploration of roundabout routes.

3.1 Dealing with graphs

It's now time to tackle the problem discussed at the end of Section 2.2, that of dealing with graphs in which we may revisit states. So far, we've been dealing with search trees where there are no loops from one state to a state that has been visited earlier. This makes our life easier, but it isn't the case in most problems. Most problem definitions allow you to revisit a state that you've already been to. For instance, issuing the observer command in SearchLab:

```
show neighbours "bristol"
```

(which lists the towns that are adjacent to Bristol) gives the response:

```
[["london" 119] ["exeter" 77] ["shrewsbury" 134] ["oxford" 73]
["southampton" 76] ["birmingham" 85]]
```

So we can get to six towns from Bristol, including Exeter, yet Exeter is not shown as a possible successor of Bristol in Box 2.2. Figure 2.10 shows an updated version of Figure 2.8 that contains all the previously visited towns in the successors of each town.

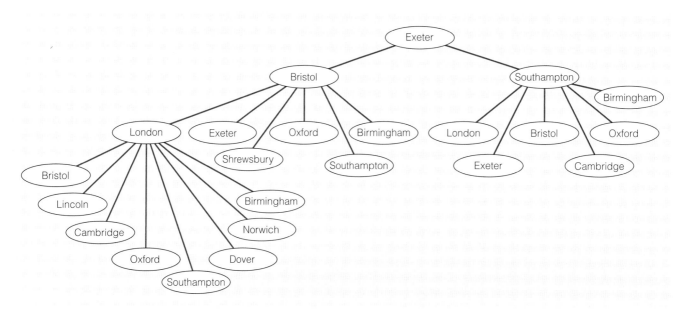

Figure 2.10   The search tree of Figure 2.8 with the already-visited nodes included

SAQ 2.4

How would you expect depth-first search to explore this search tree? How about breadth-first search?

ANSWER...

Depth-first search would get stuck in an infinite loop, moving from Bristol to London and back to Bristol. Breadth-first search would revisit the previously visited towns and expand them, but it would still make progress on the new paths and would eventually find a route from the start to the goal.

As this exercise shows, revisiting already-expanded states is at best inefficient and at worst disastrous. What we need is a way of identifying states we've already visited so that we don't go to the bother of visiting them again. There are four ways of doing this:

1   Change the operators in the problem so that no states are generated that have already been visited. While this is a nice idea in practice, it will be virtually impossible to implement and will severely limit the flexibility of the problem solver (if Exeter is not listed as a neighbour of Bristol, how would the system find a route from Bristol to Exeter?). This approach is basically never used in practice.

2   Don't include a node's parent as one of its successors. This has the advantage of being simple to implement and inexpensive to perform. It would eliminate the Bristol–London loop but it wouldn't prevent a depth-first search algorithm getting stuck in longer cycles, such as Exeter–Bristol–Southampton.

3   Don't include any potential successors if they're already in this path. This method eliminates the danger of longer cycles but it still leaves room for duplication of effort. For instance, when using breadth-first search to move from Exeter to Manchester, London will be expanded twice (once for the Exeter–Bristol–London route and once for Exeter–Southampton–London). If all we're interested in is whether a goal is reachable or not, we don't need this duplication.

4   Don't expand any node that has already been expanded. We can implement this by having both an agenda (an **open list** of nodes awaiting expansion) and a **closed list** (of nodes that we don't want to expand). Whenever a node is expanded, we place it on the closed list. This prevents any duplication of effort, but it can be more expensive to perform if the closed list becomes large.

Exercise 2.4

How do these techniques address the completeness and complexity of breadth-first and depth-first search? As you should recall, a search algorithm is complete if it always finds a solution if one exists.

Discussion ....

Breadth-first search is already complete on any graph, so none of these techniques are needed for that reason. However, by eliminating cycles, these techniques can reduce its complexity.

Techniques 3 and 4 would eliminate cycles from the graph, and this would make depth-first search complete, so long as the graph is finite. However, the path found may be very long, and require backtracking, so depth-first search remains inefficient. Infinite graphs remain a problem for depth-first search.

In SearchLab, I'll use method 3. It gives a good balance between usefulness, efficiency and simplicity of implementation. I'll come back to method 4 when I discuss dynamic programming in Section 4.4.

3.2 Taming uninformed search

Uninformed search is easy to implement but it can easily waste time on spurious investigations. Clearly it would be useful if we could *tame* uninformed search in some way. There are a few ways we can do this and in this section you will examine these with the aid of SearchLab.

First I'll look at ways of keeping depth-first search under control. As you've seen, depth-first search yields a reasonable route from Exeter to Lincoln, but only manages to find a very long one from Exeter to Norwich. But a glance at the map shows that there should be a solution of only a few steps. What we'd like to be able to do is to combine the efficiency of depth-first search with the thoroughness of breadth-first. We can do this if we limit the depth to which depth-first search explores, allowing it to find the shorter solutions when they exist. This is a **depth-limited search**: only paths shorter than a certain depth limit are explored.

Computer Exercise 2.3

Now do Computer Exercise 2.3 on the course DVD, in which you will implement depth-limited search in SearchLab.

However, depth-limited search suffers from a problem: how do we know what the depth limit should be? We could guess, but the dangers of getting it wrong are severe. If the depth limit is too shallow, we may never find a solution that exists. If the limit is too deep, we could spend a lot of time exploring sections of the search space that are irrelevant before we find a shallower solution. One way out of this conundrum is to use **iterative deepening**: we use depth-limited search with a small depth limit. If that doesn't find a solution, we increase the depth limit a little and try again.

Computer Exercise 2.4

Now do Computer Exercise 2.4 on the course DVD, in which you will implement iterative-deepening search in SearchLab.

Surprisingly, iterative-deepening search doesn't explore many more nodes than breadth-first search.

Exercise 2.5

Consider the following questions:

1   How many nodes are there in a tree of depth d and branching factor b?

2   How many nodes are explored in an iterative-deepening search of a tree to depth d with branching factor b?

3   How do these numbers compare?

Discussion ....

1   There is one node at depth 0, b at depth 1, b^2 at depth 2, and so on. This means that there are $1 + b + b^2 + b^3 \ldots + b^d$ nodes in total. For $d = 4$ and $b = 10$, this means $1 + 10 + 100 + 1000 + 10\,000 = 11\,111$ nodes in total.

2   In the tree, the nodes at depth 0 are explored (d + 1) times, the nodes at depth 1 are explored d times, the nodes at depth 2 are explored (d – 1) times, ... and the nodes at depth d are explored once. For d = 4 and b = 10, this means (4 + 1).1 + (4).10 + (4 – 1).100 + (4 – 2).1000 + (4 – 3).10 000 = 12 345 nodes in total.

3   Given b = 10, iterative deepening only explores 11% more nodes than a breadth-first search to the same depth.

Finally, we can reduce the memory needed by all these search algorithms by limiting the size of the agenda. This is a variation of breadth-first search called **beam search**. It can have a great effect on the amount of space needed for a search, but at the expense of giving up the certainty of finding a solution if one exists (the only route to the solution may lie on one of the discarded candidate paths). This approach works better when combined with informed search (see Section 4 in this unit) so that the most promising candidates are preserved.

Computer Exercise 2.5

Now do Computer Exercise 2.5 on the course DVD, in which you will implement beam search in SearchLab.

3.3 Focusing search

As you've seen, uninformed search, especially depth-first search, can take rather long routes from start to goal. For instance, both depth-first and breadth-first searches find the Exeter–Bristol–London–Lincoln route of 331 miles, but they don't find the shortest route (via Birmingham instead of London, which is only 253 miles). Using depth-first search to find a route from Exeter to Norwich is even worse: it takes us on an 800-mile round tour of England, and even suggests that going via Scotland would be a good idea! Even the more reasonable route found by breadth-first search is not the shortest one in terms of total distance.

Computer Exercise 2.6

Now do Computer Exercise 2.6 on the course DVD, where you will use depth-first search and breadth-first search to find routes from Exeter to Lincoln, Exeter to Norwich and Exeter to Shrewsbury. Which of these routes seem reasonable and which are barmy?

This is a problem when we're trying to find the best (i.e. shortest) path to a goal rather than just trying to show that a path exists. Uninformed search is good at doing the latter, but not the former. This raises the question of how we can make uninformed search better able to find good routes without wasting time exploring infeasible ones. One way to do this is to ensure that the search considers promising intermediate states before the unpromising ones. It follows that we need a definition of 'promising', which in turn implies a deeper understanding of the problem area beyond simply knowing which states are reachable from others.

The first thing we'll try is to take account of the costs of the various transitions between states and try the cheapest moves first. Then we'll look a ways of trying out the best moves first.

Uniform-cost search

Take another look at how breadth-first search looks for a route from Exeter to Lincoln. It moves out from Exeter one 'layer' at a time. It eventually finds the route Exeter–Bristol–London–Lincoln. However, this isn't the shortest route: that's Exeter–Bristol–Birmingham–Lincoln. Both London and Birmingham are neighbours of Bristol, so why does breadth-first search look at routes via London before those via Birmingham? The answer is simply that London is listed before Birmingham in Bristol's list of neighbours. However, the partial route Exeter–Bristol–London is 196 miles long, while Exeter–Bristol–Birmingham is 162 miles. If we're trying to find the shortest route from Exeter to somewhere, it makes sense to examine the shortest partial routes first. This is the idea behind **uniform-cost search**: to keep the costs of all the paths on the agenda as uniform as possible, so preventing the search from being drawn into a long route while there are shorter routes to be explored. We do this by recording (or calculating) the incurred cost of each partial path on the agenda, then sorting the agenda by this incurred cost. The cheapest partial paths will move to the front of the agenda, where they will be expanded first. If we keep expanding the cheapest path in the agenda, we will find the cheapest path to any node. Once we've found a path to the goal node, we can stop because we know that we've found the shortest route to it. This is true so long as two conditions are met:

▶ The graph is locally finite (i.e. every state has a finite number of successors).

▶ Every operation used to move to a new state incurs a non-infinitesimal, positive cost. This means that even infinitely long paths will acquire arbitrarily large costs, so other paths will be explored.

These conditions mean that uniform-cost search is both complete and optimal: it is guaranteed to find the shortest path, if any path exists. However, it's inefficient.

Computer Exercise 2.7

Now do Computer Exercise 2.7 on the course DVD, where you will use SearchLab to compare uniform-cost search with breadth-first search.

SAQ 2.5

How can we be sure that we've always found the shortest path to a node? After all, when we expand the 'London' node for the first time, we'll put Lincoln on the agenda. Why doesn't the search terminate then?

ANSWER...

The search only terminates when the node being expanded is found to be the goal. If we're doing uninformed search, it doesn't matter when we detect goal nodes. However, for uniform-cost search for the shortest route to the goal, we need to be sure that all the other possible routes to the goal will be longer. If we sort the agenda by incurred cost, and a path to the goal becomes the first path on the agenda, we can be sure that every other partial path on the agenda is at least as long as the one we're expanding. This means that this path is the shortest path to the goal.

Guiding search

Another way to improve the performance of uninformed search is by altering the order in which the neighbours of each town are expanded. Have another look at the route found by depth-first search from Exeter to Norwich. Things seem to go fine up until London. Lincoln is the first neighbour of London to be expanded, so Norwich is overlooked. This leads the search off into a wild goose chase across the country. If we could ensure that Norwich is examined first, a better route would be found.

Computer Exercise 2.8

Now do Computer Exercise 2.8 on the course DVD, where you change the order in which routes are explored.

These exercises have shown that manually ordering the successors in the search tree can lead to great improvements in the performance of search. However, such adjustments are only useful for one particular combination of start and goal. If we already know what the best route to the goal is, we can arrange things so that it is found quickly. However, if we know the best route already, why do we need to bother to search?

Nevertheless, the idea of using *knowledge* about the goal to change the order in which items appear in the agenda is a powerful one. Using such knowledge to inform the search process is the theme of the next section.

Informed search

If we want to improve the performance of our search process, to find optimal (or at least good) solutions in a sensible time, it makes sense to exploit what we know about the problem to help find those solutions. The normal way to embed this knowledge in our problem-solving system is in the form of a **heuristic**. In this section, I'll look at how heuristics can be used to inform and guide search, as well as considering how heuristics can be developed.

4.1   Heuristics

A simple definition of heuristics is 'extra information that allows you to complete a task.' Sometimes heuristics are also defined as 'rules of thumb' – information that is generally, but not always true: 'elephants are bigger than people' or 'five minutes is a good time to boil an egg' are both perfectly valid heuristics. The problem with heuristics is that they may not always produce the correct answer – a child's toy elephant is smaller than most people whilst someone who likes a runny egg will find that a cooking time of five minutes is too long. Nevertheless, heuristics are useful since they can produce a solution far faster than an exhaustive search, if we accept that this solution is not guaranteed to be accurate.

All this suggests that we can use heuristics to get an approximate idea of what the solution to a problem should look like, and then use other techniques to check this, and related, solutions. For instance, in the route-planning domain, we can use the straight-line 'as the crow flies' distance to guide the selection of the next town to expand. If we're in Bristol and trying to get to Lincoln, examining routes from Birmingham would seem to be a more sensible step than moving to Exeter, as Birmingham is closer to Lincoln than Exeter.

If we can arrange the different states along some kind of dimensions (such as latitude and longitude for towns), the different heuristic values for each state will form a kind of *landscape* (see Figure 2.11). The highest point in the landscape has the highest heuristic value. If we've designed our heuristic well, this is also the optimal solution.

I can now show how to use this idea to guide search towards the goal state.

Figure 2.11   A heuristic landscape showing estimated distances to Lincoln

4.2 | Best-first search

Given a heuristic function, we can use it to select the most promising partial routes to the goal. It behaves in much the same way as breadth-first search, except that, after the agenda is updated, it is sorted so that the nodes with the best heuristic values are at the front of the agenda. These nodes are processed next, with the effect of keeping the search focused on the goal.

Computer Exercise 2.9

Now do Computer Exercise 2.9 on the course DVD, which explores best-first search.

As you saw in the exercise, best-first search does a good job of finding reasonable paths to the goal without exploring many alternative routes. However, it doesn't always find the best routes: the shortest path from Exeter to Lincoln is 253 miles (via Bristol and Birmingham), while best-first search finds a route of 340 miles (via Southampton and Cambridge).

SAQ 2.6

Why does best-first search find the sub-optimal route?

ANSWER..

It's a greedy algorithm, and it always takes the best choice it can. From Exeter, Southampton is closer to Lincoln than Bristol, so Southampton is chosen to be expanded first. Once at Southampton, Cambridge is closest to Lincoln, so that is expanded next. Bristol is never expanded, because it is never the closest town to Lincoln.

Exercise 2.6

Is best-first search complete or efficient? (We know it's not optimal.)

Discussion ....

It is not complete, as it may get drawn down a path that is infinitely long yet never gets further away from the goal than other states. So long as this doesn't happen (as in all problems where each operator has a finite cost), best-first search is complete.

Best-first search is moderately efficient, as it generally only expands those paths that lead to the goal. However, if the heuristic isn't very discriminating, best-first search can be as bad as (or even worse than) breadth-first search.

The use of a heuristic now means that we can quickly identity unpromising routes. If they're unpromising, we can safely discard them to avoid them cluttering up memory (recall that the problem with breadth-first and uniform-cost searches is the amount of memory they use to retain all the partially explored paths). The easy way to do this is to implement the beam limit of Computer Exercise 2.5.

4.3 A* search

The weakness of best-first search is that it does not take into account the cost of the path that has been explored when choosing the next node to visit. That means that although it is able to find a solution, the path to the goal may not be the cheapest. Likewise, uniform-cost search does not take into account the cost to the goal: the path it finds will be the shortest one, but it may explore a lot of alternatives before it gets there. **A* search** improves search by considering both the cost of the path that has been explored and the estimated cost of going from the current node to the goal. Mathematically, the cost of the path that has been explored is denoted by $g(n)$ and the estimated cost of going from the current node to the goal by $h(n)$, where n denotes the node that is to be visited next. The heuristic-based evaluation function, $f(n)$, employed by A* search combines $g(n)$ and $h(n)$:

$$f(n) = g(n) + h(n)$$

In another words, it calculates the cost of the path from the start node to node n and estimates the cost from node n to the goal. As with uniform-cost and best-first search, the agenda is sorted by the value of $f(n)$ and the node selected to be visited next (n) is the one with the lowest overall cost.

Computer Exercise 2.10

Now do Computer Exercise 2.10 on the course DVD, which explores A* search.

You can see more clearly how A* operates if we look in detail at how it finds the route from Exeter to Norwich. Figure 2.12 shows the first four stages of the search. In the diagram, the f score for each leaf node in the search tree is given, in the form of $g + h$. Looking at the diagram, it's easy to see that the node with the lowest f score is the one that's expanded at each stage.

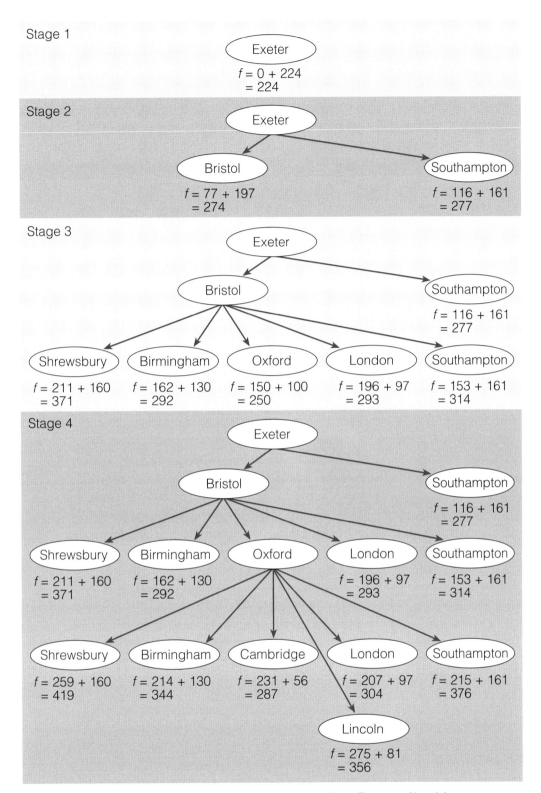

Figure 2.12 The first four stages in the search for a route from Exeter to Norwich

If we add a constraint on the form of the heuristic, we can show that A* search is complete, optimal and efficient.

A* search is complete for the same reason that uniform-cost search is complete: so long as each step along a path has a cost, infinite paths will eventually be discarded in favour of other, shorter paths.

A* is optimal so long as the heuristic used is **admissible**. Admissible heuristics are ones that always underestimate the true cost of a solution from that state. Intuitively, this is important because it means that partially constructed optimal paths will always look more alluring than all sub-optimal paths to the goal; if the heuristic sometimes overestimated the cost to the goal, this would not necessarily be the case.

The proof of optimality is quite simple. Let's say that G is a goal state and the optimal cost of getting to it is f^* ($= g^*$, since $h^* = 0$). Now imagine another goal state, G', that has a sub-optimal path to it: in other words, $g(G') > f^*$. Assume that A* has just selected G' for expansion from the agenda. Since G' is a goal state, this will terminate the search and G' will be returned. We can now show that this is impossible.

The optimal path to G cannot be fully expanded, or else the search would have already terminated. Let's call the end node of that path n. Because our heuristic, h, is admissible, we can say that:

$$f^* \geq f(n)$$

If G' is chosen for expansion over n, it must be that:

$$f(n) \geq f(G')$$

Therefore:

$$f^* \geq f(n) \geq f(G')$$

But, as G' is a goal state, $h(G') = 0$ so $f(G') = g(G')$. This means that:

$$f^* = g^* \geq g(G')$$

In other words, the cost of getting to G' is lower than the optimal cost, f^*. This is impossible, as we know that G' is a sub-optimal goal and therefore has a higher cost. That means that our assumption, that G' has been selected for expansion before n, must be false. Therefore, A* can never expand (and hence return) sub-optimal goals.

We can also show that A* is an efficient algorithm for finding these optimal routes. Indeed, there can be no other search algorithm that can find optimal paths by expanding fewer nodes than A* does. This is easiest to see if we assume that the heuristic function we're using is **monotonic**, that is that the f costs of nodes on a path always increase as the path lengthens. This is to be expected, as the heuristic we're using is admissible and so underestimates the total cost of that path. If A* is expanding a node with a given f value, we can say that it's also expanded all other nodes with a lesser f value, and may have expanded a few with the same f value. Once we've found the f value of a path to the goal, we've identified an upper bound on the f value of the optimal path. By ensuring that every partial path of lower f value has also been examined, we can be sure that we've not overlooked any better paths. This allows us to say something about the efficiency of A*. Let's imagine that we've discovered another search algorithm that expands fewer nodes than A* yet still finds a route to the goal with a particular f cost. The only way that we can find this path by expanding few nodes is by skipping some of the nodes that A* examined. This means that it's skipping some partial paths that could lead to goals with a lower f value than the one that our new algorithm has found, so our new algorithm cannot guarantee that it will find the optimal path to the goal.

If the heuristic isn't monotonic, and the f value doesn't increase along the path, we can easily turn it into one by making the f value of a node the maximum of its calculated f value and its parents' f value.

4.4   Dynamic programming

Despite our assertions that A* is efficient, in that no other optimal solution finding algorithm will expand fewer nodes, there are still ways that A* can be made more efficient. Some of these techniques are related to iterative-deepening search and beam search. However, one important area of inefficiency in A* is that it sometimes expands the same node more than once. If we take the final search tree in Figure 2.12, we see that Southampton occurs three times as a leaf node and the f value is calculated for each. This is obviously a waste of time: these nodes all represent different paths for getting to Southampton, and only one of them (the node with the lowest g value) can possibly lie on the optimal path. **Dynamic programming** is a method for avoiding this duplication of effort.

Generally speaking, for a problem to be amenable to dynamic programming the problem must have the properties of *overlapping sub-problems* and *optimal substructure*:

▶ A problem is said to have **overlapping sub-problems** if the same sub-problems can be used to solve many different larger problems. For instance, finding a good route from Oxford to Manchester is useful when looking for a good route from Southampton to Carlisle.

▶ **Optimal substructure** means that optimal solutions of sub-problems can be used to find the optimal solutions of the overall problem. For example, suppose we want to find the optimal route to travel from Bristol to Leeds via Birmingham (the overall problem), we can break down the problem into finding the optimal route between Bristol and Birmingham and Birmingham and Leeds.

During the process of finding the optimal route between Bristol and Leeds via Birmingham, small optimal sub-routes are discovered. Instead of wasting time in finding these small optimal sub-routes over and over again, we can save them and, when we need to solve the same problem later, retrieve and reuse them. This approach is called **memoisation**.

In A*, the sub-problems we come across are all in the form of a path between the start node and a particular intermediate node. These paths are recorded in a **memoisation table**. When we want to add a node (n) to the agenda, we first look it up in the memoisation table. If n isn't present, we add it to the table (together with its g cost) and to the agenda. If the node is in the table, and the table records a lower g cost than we have for n, we know that n cannot lie on the optimal path so we don't add it to the agenda. Otherwise, we add n to the agenda and move on.

As you can see from Figure 2.13, dynamic programming makes the agenda rather smaller, resulting in a more efficient search. Adding dynamic programming does not change the result of a problem-solving algorithm such as A*, but it can make it more efficient.

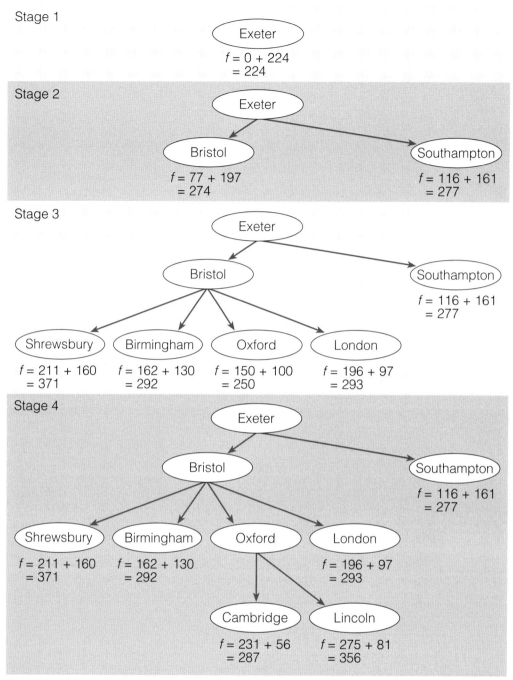

Figure 2.13   The A* search tree from Figure 2.12, with dynamic programming eliminating duplicate nodes

Computer Exercise 2.11

Now do Computer Exercise 2.11 on the course DVD, where you will compare A* with and without dynamic programming.

SAQ 2.7

Compare uninformed and informed searches. What are their advantages and disadvantages?

ANSWER...

The advantages of blind (uninformed) search are that it is intuitive and easy to implement. It does not require prior knowledge about the problem domain to guide the search. However, the disadvantages are that it is exhaustive and inefficient. For complex problems, it may not be able to find a solution within a given time limit (time complexity).

The advantages of informed search are that it uses heuristics to guide the search, and hence the search is more effective and efficient. However, its disadvantages are that it is not always simple to implement the heuristic function. The estimations of cost are not always accurate. For simple problems, the overheads (computation times and resources) used by the heuristic function are not always justified.

4.5 Hill-climbing and optimisation problems

So far, I've looked at problems where there are only a very few goal states and our task is to find the optimal sequence of steps to get to any one of these. But many problems, particularly optimisation problems, don't neatly fit this model. Problems like our room layout problem and the Travelling Salesman Problem (TSP) are examples of optimisation problems that you've met already. In an optimisation problem, the challenge is not really finding a solution: there are many of them, and they're easy to find. The challenge is finding the *best* solution from all the ones that are on offer. This is made more complex because it may not be easy to identify the best solution when we find it: there's no way to guarantee that the next solution we look at won't be better than what we've found so far. Nor, for most optimisation problems, are we really interested in how we get to the optimal solution, so we don't need to record the sequence of steps taken to reach it; we're interested in the best state, not the best path.

Given problems such as this, many of the search techniques we've found aren't really applicable. Instead, what we need to do is create some initial state and make changes to it to increase its quality.

One simple and powerful way of doing this is **hill-climbing search**. As the name implies, hill-climbing search is analogous to a person attempting to find paths to the top of the hill. The hills are defined by the score of the state, as shown in Figure 2.14. The search is a greedy one: when faced with a range of options for the next step, some good and some bad, hill-climbing search chooses the one that goes up in value the most. The approach seems sensible: if you want to get to the top of a hill quickly, keep going up the steepest slope you can find.

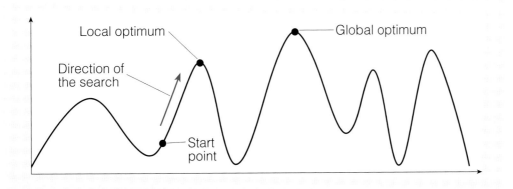

Figure 2.14   A two-dimensional search space where the start point is closer to a local optimum than to the global optimum

Hill-climbing search would seem to be an ideal way of guiding search so that optimal solutions are found quickly: the score points the way to the goal, and the search algorithm follows the most direct route there. Unfortunately, there are three serious problems with this approach:

▶ The evaluation may not give useful information about the routes to the goal. It could be that, for a wide range of nearby states, their values may be approximately equal. Again, think about this as a landscape (look back at Figure 2.11). A group of neighbouring states with more or less equal value would look like a *plateau* in this landscape. The search algorithm may spend a lot of time meandering across the plateau until it gets to a region where the evaluation function provides more information.

▶ The landscape may have ridges in it. Hill-climbing will quickly move up the steep sides of the ridge, but the ridge may slope only gently towards the solution. In this situation, the search may spend a lot of time hopping from one side of the ridge to the other, making little progress towards the goal.

▶ The most serious problem is getting trapped on a **local optimum**. This is a problem that's pervasive in all optimisation problems. Figure 2.14 shows an example of a two-dimensional view of the state space where the start point is closer to a local optimum and the search ends up at the local optimum rather than the global one. At the local optimum, all the neighbouring points have lower heuristic values than the local optimum. If the search is trying to find a definite goal, such as with route planning, it can backtrack and try another route. However, if we're just trying to find the best solution (as in the room-fitting example), we have no way of knowing that a better solution exists, so the search stops there. One way of avoiding the search being trapped at local optima is to repeat the search many times with different starting points. Hopefully, one of a number of randomly selected points will fall near the global optimum point and find the global optimum. However, for interesting problems, this can take a great deal of time. Often, the more practical approach is to lower our sights slightly and be satisfied with a good solution, even if we're not sure that it's the best one.

4.6   Developing good heuristics

So far, I've discussed heuristics, but I've said very little about what makes a good heuristic and how they are developed. I'll say a little on the subject in this section. To illustrate some of the points I'm going to make, let me introduce another example problem, the 8-puzzle (see Box 2.4).

Box 2.4: The 8-puzzle

This is probably a familiar toy. It consists of a square frame, three units on a side. Within the frame there are eight tiles, each one unit square. Each tile has a number on it, 1–8 (see Figure 2.15). The tiles can slide past each other, horizontally or vertically, into the empty space. The objective is to go from an initial random state (e.g. Figure 2.15(a)) to the goal, where all the tiles are in their correct places (see Figure 2.15(b)).

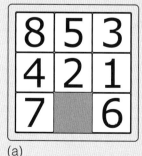
(a)

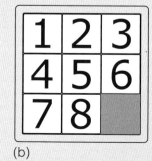
(b)

Figure 2.15   (a) The 8-puzzle. (b) Its goal state

How would you go about developing a heuristic for such a puzzle? Recall the intention of the heuristic function: it needs to assign a *score* to a state that indicates the *cost* of moving from that state to the goal. The more accurately the heuristic estimates the cost, the more accurately it will be able to guide the search towards the goal. The more accurate the heuristic, the fewer nodes will be expanded by the search.

We also have to pay attention to the time and space used by the heuristic evaluation function. The best heuristic to use would be one that always returns the real cost to the goal. An easy way to do this would be to perform an exhaustive, breadth-first or uniform-cost search from the current state to the goal and return the cost of that path. However, we've already seen that such searches are prohibitively expensive, so it isn't perhaps such a good idea. What we need is a heuristic evaluation function that is good enough, but not too expensive to calculate.

This still leaves us with the question of how to come up with candidates for heuristic evaluation functions. One way to develop such functions is to look at the constraints on the problem and relax them, resulting in an easier problem. This should be easier to solve, and so should mean that we can generate an answer quickly, which will bear some relation to the true cost of the solution.

To illustrate this, consider the 8-puzzle problem. There are clear constraints on how we can move the tiles:

1   Tiles can only move into an empty square.

2   Tiles can only move horizontally and vertically.

3   Tiles can only move one space at a time.

If we eliminate one or more of these constraints, we will end up with a simpler problem. For the 8-puzzle, there are three alternatives:

1   Most of the difficulty of the puzzle comes from Constraint 1. Whenever we want to move a tile from one position to another, we always have to worry about moving other tiles from that position. If we relax this constraint, allowing tiles to overlap, the puzzle becomes much easier. We can solve it by moving each tile independently to its correct position, and the cost of moving each tile is simply the number of spaces horizontally or vertically it needs to move. For instance, looking at Figure 2.15(a), Tile 1 needs to move up one space and across two, giving a cost of three. We call the distance from point A to point B, when travel can only be horizontal or vertical, the **Manhattan distance**.

2   If we relax Constraint 2 as well, the tiles can move directly towards their goal position and the cost of moving each tile is the **Euclidean distance**. For instance, the cost of putting Tile 1 in position will be $\sqrt{(2^2 + 1^2)} = 2.23$.

3   If we relax Constraints 1 and 3, we can move tiles simply to the correct positions with a cost of one.

Exercise 2.7

What would each of these three heuristic functions return for the position shown in Figure 2.15(a)?

Discussion ....

Alternative 1 evaluates to 3 + 1 + 0 + 0 + 1 + 1 + 0 + 3 = 9.

Alternative 2 evaluates to 7.46.

Alternative 3 evaluates to 5, since there are five tiles out of position.

Given that we have a range of heuristic functions, which should we use? If they all take a similar time to evaluate, we should obviously take the more accurate one. If we're using A* search, we need to ensure that whatever heuristic we use is admissible. If the heuristics take different times to evaluate, and time is important, then we have a more complex decision to make. There are no hard-and-fast rules here and we generally have to make an engineering trade-off between the amount of time spent evaluating heuristics against the amount of time spent expanding nodes unnecessarily. The right decision will depend on the exact details of the problem at hand.

Computer Exercise 2.12

Now do Computer Exercise 2.12 on the course DVD, where you will compare different heuristics (and different searches) for the 8-puzzle.

5 Games and adversarial search

So far, I've only considered problems that involve a single agent trying to find a solution to a problem. But in Unit 1, I said that chess has long been considered *the* problem that has interested Symbolic AI researchers. How can we apply the lessons we've learnt from our study of search techniques so far to games that involve two (or more) players, usually at odds with each other?

5.1 Adversaries and minimax

Some games, such as the 8-puzzle or solitaire, are single-player games, so the search techniques I've discussed are fully capable of playing them. More interesting games involve two or more people competing against each other. Such games are **adversarial**: what is good for one player is bad for another.

The progress of games can easily be represented as search trees: nodes represent the state of a game (the layout of the board, cards in hand, or whatever) and the operations are the legal moves. Games normally have clear winning positions and fixed starting positions, so identifying starting and finishing states is easy. The difficulty is to include the opposing goals of the different players.

Generating the game tree is easy. First, at the starting player's turn we can enumerate all their possible moves, giving a set of states reachable from the start position at the first turn. Now it is the second player's turn, and we take each of these states and determine all the possible responses the second player could make in that state. Returning to the first player, for each of the possible results of the second player's turn, we determine the first player's possible responses, and so on until we generate the entire game tree. This produces a tree like that shown in Figure 2.13. This tree is organised in layers. In each layer (called a **ply**), one player is active. A sequence of plies where every player is active once is called a **move**, so for two-player games there are two plies for each move. For games with more than two players (such as bridge or ludo), there are more plies per move. In this section I will just consider two-player games.

SAQ 2.8

If a chess-playing program can find a checkmate (winning) position in three moves, how many plies are there in the search tree?

ANSWER...

Chess is a two-player game, so three moves implies that there are six plies in the search tree.

Most games give each player several options for their turn and games take many moves to resolve. This is generally what's required for an interesting game, but it leads to game trees that are far too large to be easily drawn.

Exercise 2.8

Draw the first two plies of the game tree for noughts and crosses. How big a piece of paper would you need to draw the whole game tree (down to nine plies)?

Discussion ....

I admit, I cheated by not drawing out the entire tree for the second ply (I expect you did too). The first ply contains nine nodes, the second $9 \times 8 = 72$ nodes, the third $9 \times 8 \times 7 = 504$ nodes. The whole tree contains at most 3^9 nodes. If each node needs 3 cm^2 for display (including space for arrows), the whole tree will need 3×3^9 cm^2 = 59 049 cm^2, about two and a half metres a side. And that's for just a simple game like noughts and crosses.

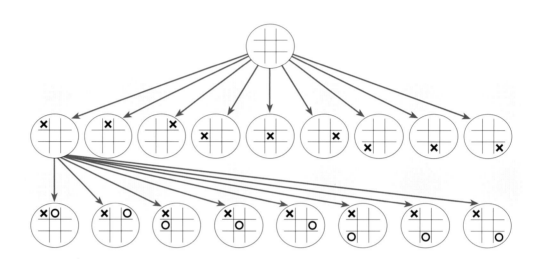

Figure 2.16 The beginning of a game tree for noughts-and-crosses

To keep our examples tractable, I'll base my discussion on a very simple, two-player game called Stone. Stone is a simplified version of Nim and the rules are in Box 2.5.

Box 2.5: Rules of Stone

Stone is a game for two players. Play starts with a pile of n stones. The players take turns to remove any number of stones between one and m from the pile. Whoever takes the last stone from the pile loses.

A typical game of Stone has $n = 7$ and $m = 3$ (that is, there are initially seven stones in the pile and players can take one, two or three stones). We'll write this as Stone(7, 3). I'll use other instances of Stone as examples.

The game tree of Stone(5, 3) is shown in Figure 2.17. In this figure, the triangles contain the number of stones still in the pile. Thus, 5-2-0 is a loss for player 2; 5-2-1-0 is a loss for player 1, and so on. Note that this tree has only 28 nodes in six plies but is already on the verge of being too large to be usefully drawn out. (I won't show the game tree for Stone(7, 3), as that contains 96 nodes.)

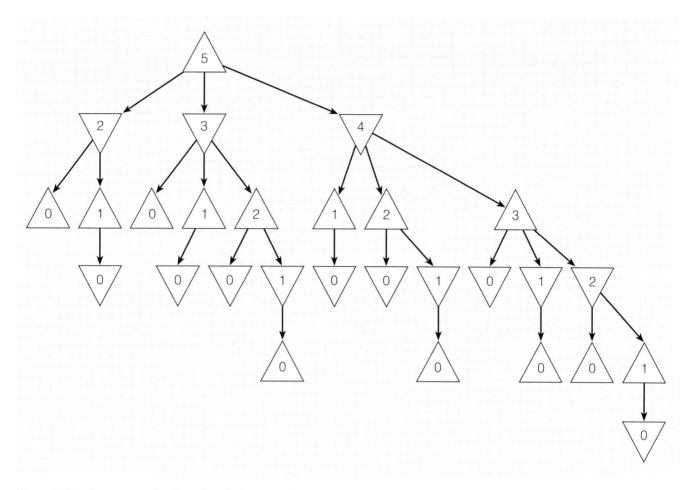

Figure 2.17   A game tree for Stone(5, 3). States before player 1's move are shown as triangles; states before player 2's move are inverted triangles

Now that we have a game tree, we can start work on developing a strategy for playing games. Each path in the game tree, from root to leaf, represents the entirety of a possible game. The leaf node represents the final state of the game, such as a win, loss, draw or the scores. The objective of a game-playing system is to select the move which will lead to the most favourable outcome for the player whose turn it is, taking into account the possible actions of the opponent. We assume that the opponent is rational and will always make the best move open to them. What we have to do is to determine what our first turn should be to ensure that we end up winning the game.

Our first step needs to be coming up with some way of evaluating the outcome of a game. In Stone, the outcomes are 'win' or 'lose' which we can give values of +1 and –1, respectively. Games like Scrabble give each player a score, which can be used to evaluate game end positions. We will call the two players MIN and MAX: MAX's objective is to finish the game with as high a score as possible, while MIN's objective to finish the game with the smallest score possible. If we know the scores of all the children of a node in the game tree, we can predict what MIN's or MAX's move would be. This allows us to assign the score of the chosen child to this node, which can be used to determine the choice made in the parent node. This is the basis of the **minimax** algorithm. I'll show how the algorithm works by looking at the smaller example search tree for a game of Stone(4, 2) (see Figure 2.18).

We start by determining the values, for MAX, of all the leaf nodes. The leaves where MAX wins are assigned a value of +1; those where MIN wins get a value of –1 (see Figure 2.18(a)). Once we know the values of all the children of a node, we can assign a value to that node. For instance, node A in Figure 2.18(b) only has one child so takes that value (+1). Node B in Figure 2.18(c) has two children. As this is a node representing MAX's turn, MAX will take the choice with the highest eventual value, so we can assign the value of +1 to node B. In Figure 2.18(d), we assign the value of −1 to node C as this is MIN's turn and she will make the move that yields the lowest eventual value. As this yields a value of −1 for the root node, we can see that a game of Stone(4, 2) always results in a loss for the first player (assuming optimal play for both players).

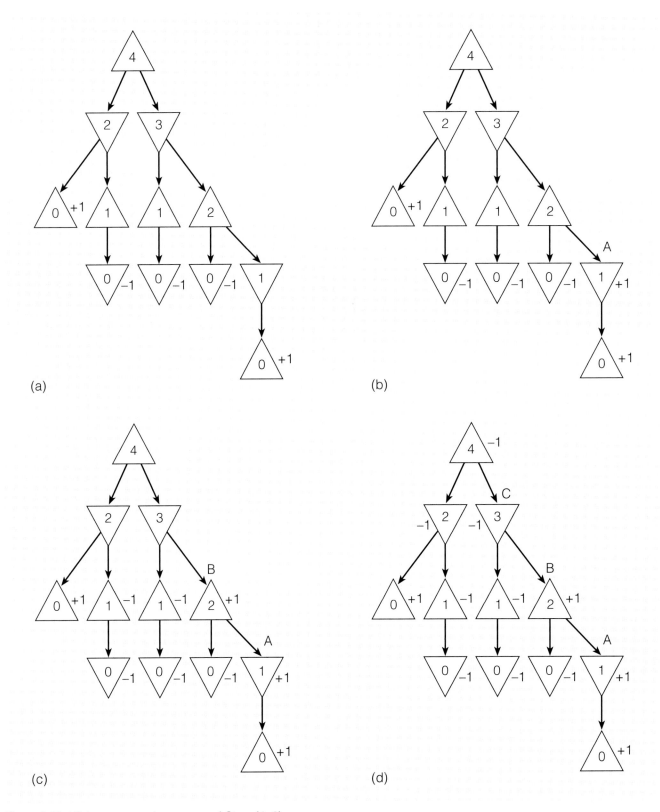

Figure 2.18 Minimax scores for a game of Stone(4, 2)

Exercise 2.9

Apply the minimax algorithm to the game tree for Stone(5, 2) (see Figure 2.19). Which player wins?

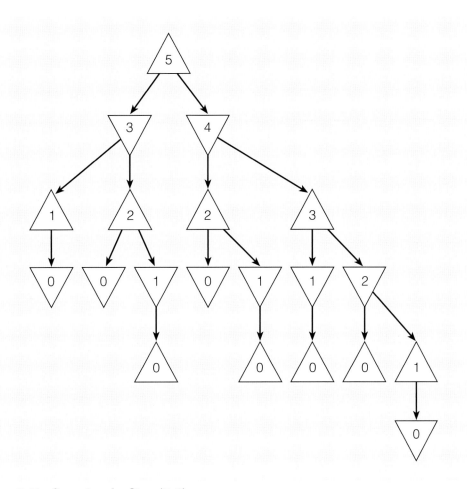

Figure 2.19   Game tree for Stone(5, 2)

Discussion ....

MAX, by taking one stone initially (see Figure 2.20).

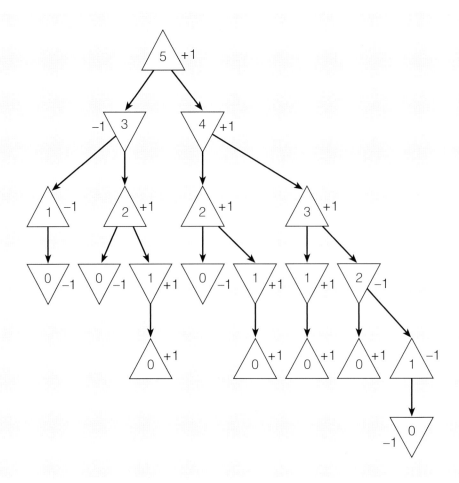

Figure 2.20   Minimax scores for a game of Stone(5, 2)

The minimax algorithm as presented here works well for simple games, but it is too naive for most games (and all the interesting ones). Minimax is based on three assumptions about games which are not true in many occasions.

▶ *Perfect information.* In many games – Stone, chess and ludo, for example – each player has 'perfect information': each player knows everything there is to know about the state of the game. In a perfect information game, each player knows what moves will be available to all of the other players, and the game tree can be built on that basis. Imperfect information games, on the other hand, hide some information from other players. Many card games, like bridge and poker, belong to this category. In these games, one player cannot predict exactly what moves the other player can make. Often, a large part of the challenge in these games lies in the attempts to deduce the hidden information and hence build a reasonable game tree.

▶ *Determinism.* The games I've looked at so far are deterministic: the moves available in any state are determined solely by the state of the game. Non-deterministic games – backgammon, say – involve an element of chance (usually by rolling dice). As in imperfect information games, non-determinism makes the game more difficult to predict and so makes finding the optimal play strategy more difficult.

I won't deal with either of these problems in this unit, but their basic effect is to make the game tree bigger, to accommodate all the options possible in the game. This simply makes the next problem worse.

▶ *Exhaustive generation.* The minimax algorithm relies on the ability to find all the terminal (leaf) nodes in the game tree, determine their scores and then back these values up to the internal nodes of the tree. But, as we saw in Unit 1, interesting games like chess have immense game trees, which are simply impossible for even the fastest computer to generate.

SAQ 2.9

Given that chess has a branching factor of 35, and it takes one millisecond to identify a move and calculate its effect, how many plies of a game tree can a chess computer generate in three minutes? How many plies could be generated with a computer ten times faster (each state takes 1 millisecond to generate)?

ANSWER...

A search tree containing n plies has 35^n nodes. In three minutes, the computer can generate $3 \times 60 \times 1000 = 180\,000$ nodes. We need to find n such that $35^n = 180\,000$.

Taking logs of both sides:

$$\log 35^n = \log 180\,000$$
$$n \log 35 = \log 180\,000$$
$$n = \log 180\,000 \,/\, \log 35$$
$$n = 3.4$$

So our chess computer would not even be able to look two complete moves (four plies) ahead.

If we have a computer that is ten times faster, the number of plies explored is:

$$
\begin{aligned}
n &= (\log 180\,000 * 10) \,/\, \log 35 \\
&= (\log 180\,000 + \log 10) \,/\, \log 35 \\
&= \log 180\,000 \,/\, \log 35 + \log 10 \,/\, \log 35 \\
&= 3.4 + \log 10 \,/\, \log 35 \\
&= 3.4 + 0.64 \\
&= 4.04
\end{aligned}
$$

So we need to generate 10 000 states per second to be able to look ahead two moves in chess in three minutes. We would need another factor of 100 speed-up (i.e. generating one million states per second) to generate a game tree of five plies. Given that an average player looks ahead six to eight plies, we can see that we have quite a problem to deal with.

This strategy of exhaustive search is often feasible for the opening and closing stages of a game, particularly chess. In both these stages, there may be very few states or moves to consider so pre-computing and storing these 'books' of optimal moves is a viable approach.

Since it's obvious that for any interesting game we won't be able to explore anything like the entire game tree, we have to adopt strategies that explore as much of the interesting parts of it that we can. The first tactic is simply to throw more processing power at the problem: use more and faster processors to churn through more states in the game tree. Optimising the algorithms we use for the search can also increase the number of states we can examine in a unit time. However, this strategy can only take us so far: the size of the game tree will always be massively larger than could be processed by any feasible machine.

The other tactic is to exploit *intelligence*, in the shape of meta-knowledge, while exploring the game tree, focusing our search on the parts of the game tree that are most likely to lead to good moves. As before, a heuristic function returns the expected value of the nodes generated, and this information is used to make a best guess at a good move.

5.2 Evaluation functions and the horizon problem

The minimax algorithm remains the basis of our game-playing strategy here. The basic tree exploration system generates the game tree to a depth of a few plies. If we can evaluate to the nodes at the leaves of this partial tree, we can use minimax to select the best move based on these evaluations.

This raises the question of what our evaluation function should look like. As we're using it in minimax, we're using the evaluation function simply to rank the nodes so that minimax can select the node with either the highest or the lowest value. This suggests that we don't have to be too fussy about the precise value given to a state by the evaluation function, so long as the ranking of states is accurate. This vagueness about the evaluation function has another benefit: approximately right evaluation functions are likely to be faster to calculate.

SAQ 2.10

Why is it important that the evaluation function is quick to calculate?

ANSWER..

The evaluation function needs to be calculated for every node generated in the game tree. If it takes too long to calculate, the game player will be unable to explore many nodes in the tree.

While we've said that the evaluation function need not be totally accurate, it's important that the ranking it produces is correct over all the nodes explored in the game tree. One way this is achieved in practice is to give many nodes the same evaluation, declaring that we can't (from a quick look) really choose between them. For instance, chess positions could be evaluated by looking at the values of all the pieces (each piece in chess is given a value based on how useful it is). Simply adding up the values of all the pieces on each side is quick and a significant advantage in pieces is also quite a reliable prediction of how likely a player is to win. However, it does not take into account most of the tactical considerations, such as pins and forks, described in Unit 1, Section 7.1, so it cannot be totally accurate. This is easy to see when we consider that a great many positions, of different tactical strength, will have the same evaluation. However, the best computer chess systems use very sophisticated evaluation functions, based on grandmaster play: the 'intelligence' of the system lies in these.

There is, nevertheless, a significant problem with relying on evaluation functions to choose the best move: the function will only judge the value of a state, but it cannot evaluate states that follow from it. For instance, a position like that shown in Figure 2.21 (a) shows a large material advantage for black. If this was found at the limit of a search, it might be selected by white as an unfavourable position to be avoided. However, this position is actually a terrific one for white, as white's next move is simply to move the knight from e5 to f7 – checkmate.

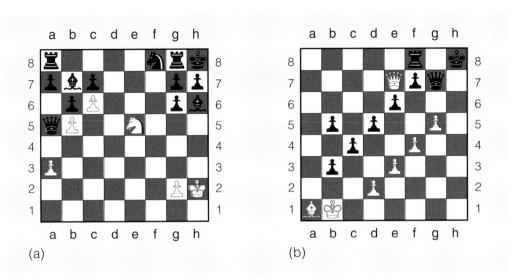

Figure 2.21   Two examples of the horizon problem in chess

This inability to see the consequences of moves is known as the **horizon problem**. It is a consequence of the search only being able to look a limited number of plies into the game tree. It's obvious in the position shown in Figure 2.21(b) (black to move). The white bishop on a1 (bishops move diagonally) threatens the black queen on g7. The queen can't move away, because to do so would expose the king on h8 to attack. However, black can delay the capture by advancing one of the pawns, which would block the bishop's line of attack. However, this will only delay the inevitable: each pawn that is moved will be immediately captured by the bishop, restoring the threat on the queen. The black queen will be captured either by the bishop or, if it captures the bishop, by one of the pawns or the king. A human player can see that the capture is inevitable and move to position himself for the aftermath; a computer system exploring the game tree to anything less than ten plies simply won't see it.

This problem can be reduced by trying to identify those game states where things could change rapidly and extending the exploration from those nodes, at the expense of not exploring so deeply from nodes that seem more static. However, adjusting the search algorithm in this way will never eliminate the horizon problem: the problem is inherent in using search for game playing. The more effective way that this problem can be tackled is by changing the representation of the game to one that includes more strategic considerations, such as the ones described in Unit 1, Section 7.1. If concepts like pins and forks are included in the evaluation function, poor moves can be identified more quickly and the game player's resources can be focused more effectively.

5.3 | Efficiency gains: α-β pruning

The notion of focusing effort on those parts of the game tree that are worth exploring brings us to the idea of **pruning**. Given that there is only a limited number of nodes we can explore while considering a move, we don't want to waste time exploring the consequences of moves that are obviously bad for us. For instance, in Figure 2.21(a) white has many moves available but one of them (Nf7) leads to checkmate. In this situation, we must assume white will make this move, so it is a waste of time exploring the consequences of the other moves available to white from this state. In other words, we *prune* the search tree to eliminate branches that will never be taken in actual play. We can check whether a branch is reachable by keeping track of two parameters, imaginatively called α (alpha) and β (beta). MAX can force the game to be worth at least α, while MIN can force the game to be no better than β. States between these values are worth exploring; states outside them are not and can be pruned.

Let's look at an example game tree (see Figure 2.22) to see how this works. Remember that the triangle nodes are MAX's choices, and she will choose the child with the highest minimax value; inverted triangles are MIN's choices, and he will choose the child with the lowest minimax value. In this game tree, the evaluations of the leaf nodes are shown in the square boxes, but these states will only be generated when they're needed. When a state is generated, it is immediately evaluated and the minimax evaluation propagated up the tree.

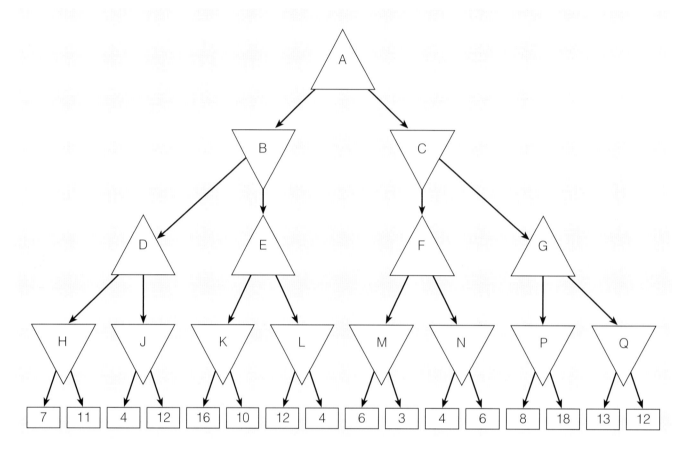

Figure 2.22   A sample game tree

Minimax uses a depth-first search of this tree, so the first sequence of moves we'll consider is A-B-D-H. H is a move for MIN, so we can assign the value of 7 to node H. We then move to consider D's other child, J. The first of J's children has a value of 4. As J is a MIN node, we know that, whatever the value of J's other children, MIN will choose a value no higher than 4 for J. As this value is lower than the minimax value of H (7), MAX will always prefer H over J, so we don't need to explore any more of J's children. D gets a minimax value of 7 (see Figure 2.23). As MAX can always force the minimax value of D to be at least 7, we'll record 7 as the α value of D and it will be passed back up to B and used when exploring E and its successors.

Now we've got the idea of α-β pruning, we can say a few things about it:

▶ Exploring the children of a MAX node can never decrease that node's α value (but can increase it).

▶ Exploring the children of a MIN node can never increase that node's β value (but can decrease it).

The minimax value of a MAX node is the highest minimax value of its children. Similarly, the minimax value of a MIN node is the lowest minimax value of its children. Also, if the α value of a node is ever greater than or equal to its β value, that node will never be reached in actual play and its other children can be pruned.

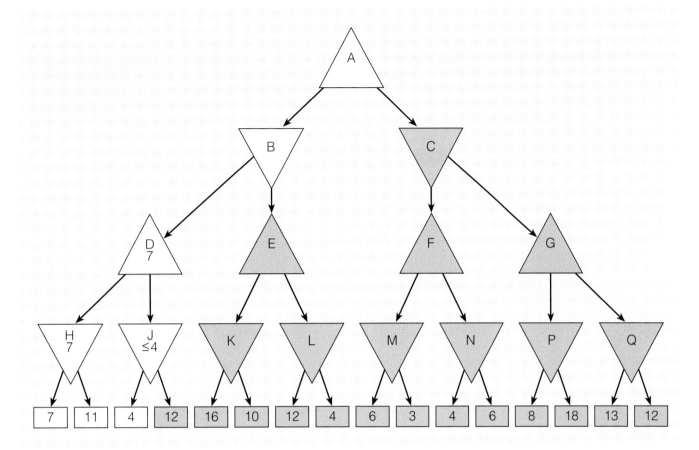

Figure 2.23   Partial evaluation of the game tree. Shaded nodes have not been evaluated

We can now write down how the α-β pruning procedure is incorporated into the minimax algorithm. It's most clearly expressed in the pseudo-code shown in Box 2.6.

Box 2.6: Minimax with α-β pruning

```
function MinimaxValueOfGame (game)
   ValueOfMax (Root (game), game, −∞, ∞)
end

function ValueOfMax (state, game, α, β)
  if Terminal (state) then return ValueOf (state)
  for each s in successors (state, game) do
     set α (Max [ α, ValueOfMin (s, game, α, β)])
     if α ≥ β then return β
  end
  return α
end

function ValueOfMin (state, game, α, β)
  if Terminal (state) then return ValueOf (state)
  for each s in successors (state, game) do
     set β (Min [ β, ValueOfMax (s, game, α, β)])
     if α ≥ β then return α
  end
  return β
end
```

When J's first successor is evaluated, J's β value is updated to its value (4). This is less than J's α value (inherited from its parent, D), so J's other successors are pruned and J's α value is returned to D.

SAQ 2.11

Look at Figure 2.24. Check that D has the correct minimax value. If the game ends up in state D, can MAX ensure that the game always ends up with a value of at least 7?

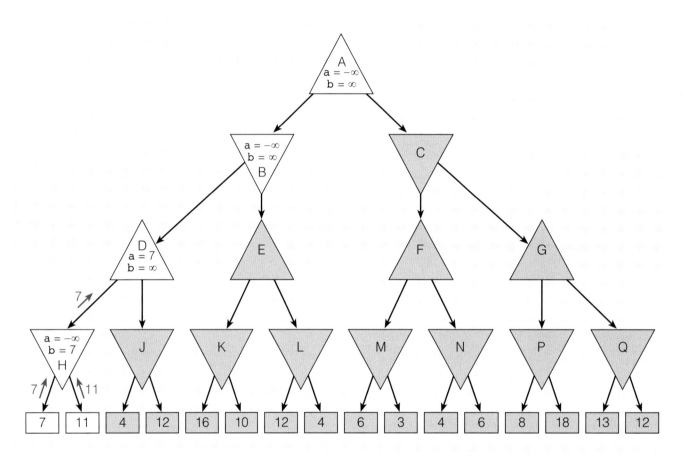

Figure 2.24   α and β values in a search tree. Shaded nodes have not been evaluated

With all of D's successors explored, its α value is passed up to B, where it becomes B's β value to reflect MIN's knowledge that a game played from B cannot have a value higher than 7. This β value is passed down to E and K. Neither of the successors of K is better for MIN than any nodes already found, so K's β value is passed back to E as K's minimax value. This value becomes E's new α value. E's α and β values are now the same, reflecting the fact that MAX can make a game played from E better than a game played from D, so MIN will always choose D over E. This is enough information to prune away the other successors of E (i.e. L). B's β value doesn't change and is returned to A as B's minimax value. This is shown in Figure 2.25.

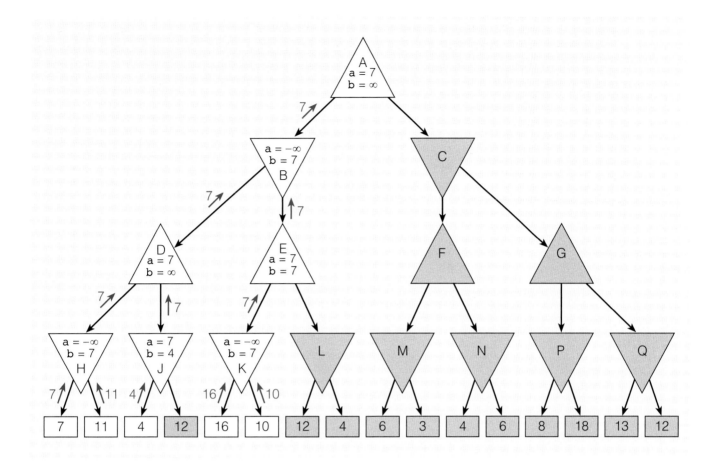

Figure 2.25   Alpha and beta values in a search tree. Shaded nodes have not been evaluated

Exercise 2.10

Continue the minimax search with α-β pruning down the other successor of A. Check that you get the same minimax value for A and that you prune the right branches.

Discussion ....

A's minimax value is 7. The completed game tree is shown in Figure 2.26. By using α-β pruning, we've eliminated 13 of the 31 nodes from consideration without needing to expand them.

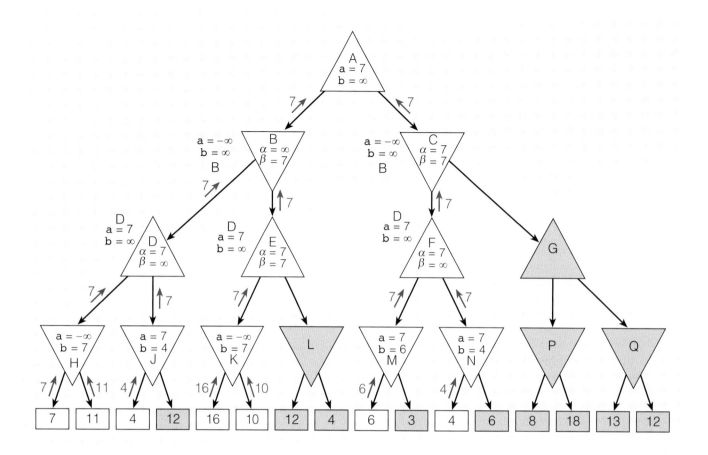

Figure 2.26 A fully examined search tree with α-β pruning. Shaded nodes have not been evaluated

This brief discussion of game-playing techniques should have shown some of the difficulties in incorporating intelligence in AI systems. α-β pruning is a relatively simple technique used to eliminate infeasible sections of the state space from exploration. As such, it represents another application of meta-knowledge to intelligence.

6 Summary of Unit 2

In this unit, I have outlined the background to the issue of search and stated why we need search as a form of reasoning with representations. Some of the terminologies of search have been explained; and I have presented examples of typical uninformed and informed search techniques, most of them intelligent route-finding and game-playing systems. You will have carried out a number of activities designed to help you to understand the search concepts I've discussed.

Games have long been a staple problem in AI research. There are many reasons for this. One is that games are relatively simple formal systems, so they are easy to encode in computers. Another is that games require few resources to play and the outcome is easily observable and quantifiable. In Unit 3 I will discuss how research into game playing has led to other advances in AI, particularly in machine learning.

Now, look back at the learning outcomes for this unit and check if you understand each of them. If necessary, revisit any section of the unit.

Unit 3: Symbolic AI in the world

CONTENTS

Introduction to Unit 3

In the previous two units I've given quite a detailed account of the two main conceptual principles of Symbolic AI: *representation* and *search*. Some of this discussion may have seemed rather abstract, so it's legitimate to ask how these principles have been applied to real problems requiring intelligent solutions. How good has Symbolic AI's track record been here? What sort of problems has it been applied to, and with what success?

I have far too little space to present a comprehensive picture of Symbolic AI's achievements and failures. Instead, I will start with what seems a quintessentially intelligent activity, *planning*, the generation of schedules of tasks that together achieve a certain aim. In Section 2, I introduce the typical Symbolic AI approach to planning that originated in an early system called STRIPS, and describe in some detail how STRIPS planning works. This discussion naturally involves the concept of a *microworld*, which I define and criticise.

If the Symbolic AI project is to be rated as any kind of success, it has to produce systems that are robust enough, *intelligent* enough, to function outside the laboratory. Section 3 looks briefly at the progress of robotic technology, starting with the granddaddy of all robots, Shakey – Stanford Research Institute's first autonomous system – through to some of the mobile vehicles and rovers of today.

Two other capacities seem also to be essential to intelligence: *learning* and working with *uncertainty*. In Section 4 I deal with the problem of learning and look at a few systems that discover new knowledge and develop their own heuristics for dealing with complex situations. Section 5 discusses symbolic approaches to uncertainty, founded on statistical ideas, such as Bayes's Theorem and fuzzy logic. I will invite you to reflect on the validity of the symbolic approach, both to machine learning and to handling uncertainty.

What you need to study this unit

You will need the following course components, and will need to use your computer and internet connection for some of the exercises.

▶   this Block 2 text
▶   the course DVD.

LEARNING OUTCOMES FOR UNIT 3

After studying this unit you will be able to:

3.1 write a set of bullets outlining the major techniques through which Symbolic AI systems can be made to learn how to make decisions and deal with uncertain information;

3.2 write a set of bullet points outlining the major features of Blocks World, and explain why it is an example of a microworld;

3.3 describe how planning systems operate, particularly STRIPS-based planners;

3.4 write a paragraph describing the successes and failures of robots in the real world;

3.5 write a few sentences outlining how decision trees can be learnt from data;

3.6 write a paragraph describing how heuristics can guide the automatic discovery of new knowledge.

2 Planning

You may recall that in Unit 2 of this block, I mentioned the problem of arranging my holiday trip to Lancashire. I have to leave home on a certain date, get to my bed and breakfast in Lancashire, spend a week visiting various attractions (not forgetting the British Lawnmower Museum) and then return home on a certain date a week later. What I need is a *plan*. As I've suggested already, planning and executing complex tasks – anything from an intricate airline schedule to a straightforward trip to the local shop and back – seems to be a classic example of intelligent activity.

At first glance, **planning** might appear to be just another form of problem solving. This is true in a way, but there are certain differences. In Symbolic AI, problem solving consists of setting a system to an initial state, defining a goal state and then defining all of the possible actions our system can take. The system will search through the space of possible states looking for a solution.

To take another simple example, consider solving the problem of buying apples from a shop. The initial state is being at home with no apples, the goal state is being back at home with some apples. Between the two lies a state space that may be something like the one shown in Figure 3.1.

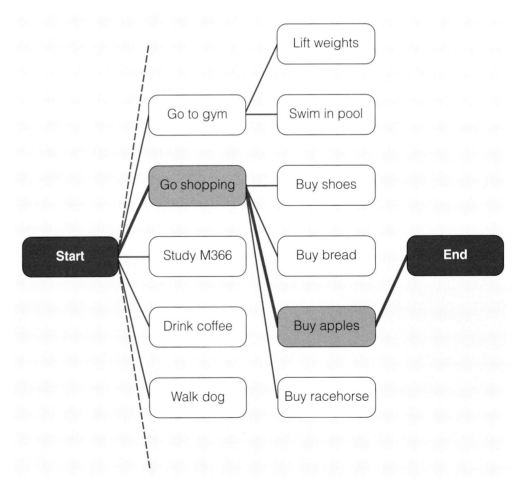

Figure 3.1 A partial search tree for the buying apples problem

But this is a grossly oversimplified picture of the problem: in reality, each level of the tree ought to have thousands, if not millions, of branches and the tree itself might have hundreds of levels. Exhaustive search of such a space is clearly infeasible, so heuristic techniques have to been brought in to speed up searches – a good heuristic would tell the system that shopping is a good way of acquiring new items (including apples). The search could then be directed along the shopping branch. A further heuristic might then guide the search towards shops that sell fruit. Of course this solution merely exchanges one problem (the scale of the search) for another (creating useful heuristics). But a more serious difficulty is that it forces the system to start either at the initial state or at the goal state and work towards the other: the search program must examine each of the initial actions before moving on to the next.

By comparison, planning relies on making direct connections between states and actions. Computers describe plans which are composed of states, goals and actions using a system of formal logic. 'Have some apples' is an English language description of a goal; the logical expression *Have(apples)* is its equivalent. Actions are described in the same manner, but also include information about the preconditions that must exist before they can be carried out and the conditions that will exist after they have been completed.

SAQ 3.1

Can you think of some preconditions that must exist for you to buy some apples?

ANSWER...

Amongst many others, you must be at a shop that sells apples, the shop must be open, they must have apples in stock and you must have some money.

In fact, it is quite astonishing how many preconditions there are for even the simplest action. In the exercise above, I only identified a few very simple ones, but countless other facts that might affect our ability to complete an action. Most AI planning systems are therefore built to handle quite limited and abstract worlds, which offer a greatly restricted set of possibilities. I shall return to look at an example of one of these simplified worlds in our discussion of the Blocks World in Section 2.

Returning to our apple-buying plan, the planning system will include a general action *Buy(x)* – where x is an item. The result of *Buy(x)* is that you now have x – written as *Have(x)*. Ignoring the preconditions, like having money, being in the shop, etc., we can write the process as shown in Table 3.1.

Table 3.1 Possible planning system for buying apples

	Initial condition	Action	Result
General form	¬*Have(x)*	*Buy(x)*	*Have(x)*
In English	'I don't have x'	'I buy x'	'I have x'
Specific example	¬*Have(apples)*	*Buy(apples)*	*Have(apples)*
In English	'I don't have any apples'	'I buy apples'	'I have some apples'

If the planner's goal includes the condition *Have(apples)*, then it can determine that an appropriate plan to achieve that goal should somewhere include the action *Buy(apples)*.

A second key aspect of planning is that it does not enforce the order in which the plan is evaluated. Continuing our example, a planner may decide the action *Buy(apples)* before it has determined where to get the apples or what to do afterwards. Once the action

Buy(apples) has been added to the plan, the planner can add new actions. An obvious choice would be to compare the preconditions of Buy(x) with the planner's current state. The planner would then realise it needed to go shopping to satisfy Buy(x)'s preconditions, and so would add that action to the plan. This would continue until every action from the initial state to the goal state can be completed in full, at which point the plan can be executed.

Finally, the planning process allows for the problem to be broken down into independent chunks known as **sub-plans**. Imagine our plan was to buy a pair of shoes, a loaf of bread and some apples. We could decompose this into two sub-plans – one being to buy a pair of shoes, the other to go to the supermarket where we can buy both bread and apples. The sub-plan for the supermarket can also be broken down into a pair of sub-plans – a sub-plan to buy bread and another to buy apples.

There is little or no interaction between the sub-plans – buying apples does not depend on us buying shoes beforehand. Therefore, the order in which we complete the sub-plans is irrelevant – we could buy the shoes and then visit the supermarket or we could go to the supermarket and then visit the shoe store.

SAQ 3.2

The sub-plans in the example above are not entirely independent – can you think why?

ANSWER...

There are a number of reasons. The first is the constraint of money. If we spend too much money on one item we might have insufficient funds to satisfy the preconditions for the remaining Buy(x) actions. A second constraint you might have thought of is time – some shops open or close before others. If we perform the sub-plans in the wrong order then we may not be able to complete the plan as a whole.

2.1   Blocks World

We all know that the real world is an incredibly complex and chaotic place. However, considering all of these fine details can obscure the detail of how planning (and other tasks) is done. One answer might be to eliminate all the messy details by constructing a very simple world in which the planner can operate, and where its attention can be focused on the core problem, the construction of the plan.

One such simplified world has played a leading part in the development of AI systems. It is usually known as **Blocks World**. Blocks World was used as an environment for early natural language understanding systems (such as SHRDLU) and robots (particularly Shakey, which I discuss in Section 3.1). However, Blocks World is most closely linked with the problem of planning and with the early planning system, STRIPS. I will discuss STRIPS in Section 2.2.

As its name suggests, Blocks World is a tiny 'world' comprising an (infinitely large) flat table on which sit a set of children's building blocks. The blocks can be moved around and stacked on top of one another by a single robot hand. The hand can only hold one block at a time. Although Blocks World is sometimes implemented with real blocks and a real robot hand, it is most often simulated inside a computer, so all blocks are presumed to be perfectly regular, the movements of the arm infinitely precise, and so on.

Planning in Blocks World means deciding the steps required to move blocks from an initial configuration (the start state) to another configuration (the goal state). An example is given in Figure 3.2. You should be able to work out how to get to the goal state in Figure 3.2(b).

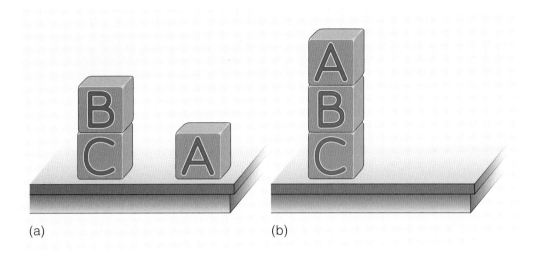

(a)   (b)

Figure 3.2   The Blocks World problem: (a) the initial state of the world. (b) the goal state of the world with the blocks neatly stacked

The states in Blocks World are described only in terms of their positions relative to one another and to the table. So the position of Block A in the state depicted in Figure 3.2(a) can be described as 'A is on the table' or more tersely *OnTable(A)*. Block B sits on top of Block C – *On(B,C)*. If we assume the robot hand is empty (*HandEmpty*) we can describe the state of the entire world as follows:

On(B,C) ∧ *OnTable(C)* ∧ *OnTable(A)* ∧ *HandEmpty*

SAQ 3.3

Use the notation above to describe the situation in Figure 3.2(b).

ANSWER..

You should have come up with an answer similar to:

On(A,B) ∧ *On(B,C)* ∧ *OnTable(C)* ∧ *HandEmpty*

It does not matter if your description of the world is in a different order to mine.

The robot hand manipulates the world by picking up blocks and moving them around. A block *x* may only be picked up if both of the following are satisfied:

▶   The robot hand is empty (*HandEmpty*).

▶   There is no block sitting on top of the selected block (*Clear(x)*).

The hand can execute simple commands – *PickUp(A)* picks up Block A, provided that the block is clear and the hand is empty; whilst *PutDown(A)* places Block A on the table provided that the hand is holding the block. A second pair of commands – *Stack(A,B)* places Block A on top of Block B provided the hand is holding A and that the top face of B is clear; *UnStack(A,B)* removes Block A from Block B provided that the hand is empty and that the top of A is clear.

SAQ 3.4

What Blocks World commands will perform the task of moving the blocks from the state in Figure 3.2(a) to the goal state in Figure 3.2(b)? Assume the robot hand is empty to start with.

ANSWER...

PickUp(A)

Stack(A,B)

2.2 Planning in the Blocks World

Imagine that we have an initial state of the Blocks World as shown in Figure 3.3(a). Blocks A and C are on the table and Block B is stacked on top of Block C. We want to end up at the goal state (see Figure 3.3(b)), where Blocks A and C are sitting on the table and B is stacked on A.

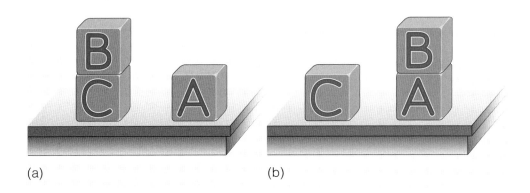

(a)   (b)

Figure 3.3 Another Blocks World problem. (a) shows the initial state of the world. (b) shows the goal state of the world where Block B is stacked on top of Block A

SAQ 3.5

Describe the initial and goal states for this problem using the notation developed above.

ANSWER..

Initial state: *On(B,C) ∧ OnTable(C) ∧ OnTable(A) ∧ HandEmpty*

Goal state: *OnTable(C) ∧ On(B,A) ∧ OnTable(A) ∧ HandEmpty*

For the remainder of this section we shall ignore the robot hand in state descriptions.

To build the plan we can decompose the problem into three sub-problems. From the initial state we want to end up with Block A on the table, Block C on the table and Block B on top of Block A. As you can see in Table 3.2, two of these sub-problems are already solved.

Table 3.2 Planning sub-problems for Figure 3.3

Initial state	*OnTable(A)*	*OnTable(C)*	*On(B,C)*
Goal state	*OnTable(A)*	*OnTable(C)*	*On(B,A)*
Solved?	Yes	Yes	No

Our planner therefore does not need to develop plans for these problems; it can concentrate on building a plan for moving Block B to its final state.

The planner knows what actions it can perform, and the consequences of those actions. Actions are expressed as *operators*. Each operator has four parts: its name, a set of preconditions, an add list and a delete list. The preconditions are those facts which must be true before the operator can be executed. The add list and delete list describe how the world changes with the execution of the operator, by specifying which facts are added to and deleted from the world state.

The operators for Blocks World are given in Table 3.3.

Table 3.3 Operators for Blocks World

Name	PickUp(x)	PutDown(x)	Stack(x,y)	UnStack(x,y)
Preconditions	HandEmpty ∧ OnTable(x) ∧ Clear(x)	Holding(x)	Holding(x) ∧ Clear(y)	HandEmpty ∧ On(x,y) ∧ Clear(x)
Add list	Holding(x)	OnTable(x) ∧ HandEmpty ∧ Clear(x)	HandEmpty ∧ On(x,y) ∧ Clear(x)	Holding(x) ∧ Clear(y)
Delete list	HandEmpty ∧ OnTable(x) ∧ Clear(x)	Holding(x)	Holding(x) ∧ Clear(y)	HandEmpty ∧ On(x,y) ∧ Clear(x)

Using these, the planning process proceeds as follows:

▶ The planner knows that the only way of achieving the state *On(B,A)* is to have performed the task *Stack(B,A)*; this is because the *Stack* operator is the only one with *On* in its add list. The operation *Stack(B,A)* is added to the end of the plan.

▶ The planner decides if the operation can be completed from the initial state. The operation *Stack(x,y)* has a pair of prerequisites – the top of the stack must be clear and the hand must be holding the block to be stacked. Examining the state of the world, the planner finds that, whilst the top of Block A is clear, the hand is not currently holding Block B. Therefore this task cannot yet be completed.

▶ The planner takes a further step back and attempts to find a solution that will satisfy the remaining prerequisite for *Stack(x,y)*. To be holding a block, the robot hand must have previously picked up the block. This can be achieved in one of two ways: if the block is on the table the arm will use *PickUp(x)*; if it is on a stack then it will use *UnStack(x,y)*. The planner re-examines the world and determines that Block B is stacked on Block C. It adds *UnStack(B,C)* to the plan.

▶ The preconditions for *UnStack(x,y)* are that the hand must be empty and the top of the block to be unstacked must be clear. In this case both prerequisites are true and *UnStack(x,y)* operation can be completed directly from the initial state.

The planner has now developed a complete plan, from initial state to goal state, in which the preconditions of each individual operation will be satisfied. The entire plan is:

Begin

UnStack(B,C)

Stack(B,A)

End

This is an example of **means–end analysis** (introduced by Newell and Simon for their General Problem Solver) – a process of working out the differences between two states and attempting to find operators that minimise the differences. Rather like backward and forward chaining, the process is centred on an *agenda* of goals to achieve. First, the goal conditions are added to the agenda. Planning then proceeds by popping the first condition from the agenda and, if it's not already true, finding an operator that can achieve it. The operator's action is then pushed on the agenda, as is each of the operator's precondition terms. Achieving each of these preconditions requires its own sub-plan. The process continues until the only things left on the agenda are actions. If these are performed, in sequence, the goals will be achieved. This algorithm is laid out in Box 3.1.

Box 3.1: The STRIPS planning algorithm

```
to achieve goals
   for each condition in goals
      add condition to agenda
   generate plan

to generate plan
   while stack not empty do
      term = pop agenda
      if term is an action then
         append action to plan
      elsif term is not already true then
         op is an operator that can achieve term
         push op onto agenda
         for each precondition of op
            push precondition onto agenda
   return plan
```

To show how this works, let's take another look at the planning problem shown in Figure 3.3. It starts with the three goal conditions being added to the agenda:

OnTable(A)

On(B,A)

OnTable(C)

The topmost term, *OnTable(A)*, is already true, so there is nothing to be done to achieve it; it's popped from the agenda and discarded. The second term is not already true, so the system finds the *Stack* operator to achieve it. *Stack(B,A)* is pushed onto the agenda and the operator's preconditions (*Clear(A)* and *Holding(B)*) are pushed on as well, giving the agenda as:

Clear(A)

Holding(B)

Stack(B,A)

OnTable(C)

and the process begins again. *Clear(A)* is already true, so that goal is discarded without action. *Holding(B)* will become true after an *UnStack(B,C)* operation, so that operator is pushed on the stack together with its preconditions. At this stage, the agenda is:

Clear(B)

On(B,C)

UnStack(B,C)

Stack(B,A)

OnTable(C)

The top two goals in the stack are true, so are popped from the agenda without further attention. The two operations (*UnStack(B,C)* and *Stack(B,A)*) are performed in that order. The final goal (*OnTable(C)*) is already true and so is removed. As the agenda is empty, all the goals have been achieved and the planning has succeeded.

This method of representing planning knowledge in operators, and creating plans by means–end analysis, was first implemented in a planning system called STRIPS (Stanford Research Institute Problem Solver). The STRIPS formalism is still widely used in planning systems and planning research.

Exercise 3.1

Show how STRIPS would generate a plan to move from the initial state to the goal state shown in Figure 3.4.

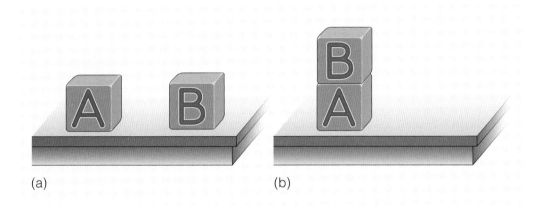

(a)   (b)

Figure 3.4   Initial and goal states for Exercise 3.1

Discussion ....

The initial state is *OnTable(A)* ∧ *OnTable(B)* ∧ *Clear(A)* ∧ *Clear(B)*. The goal state is *OnTable(A)* ∧ *On(B,A)*. The plan generated is:

PickUp(B)
Stack(B,A)

The agenda changes as shown in Box 3.2.

Box 3.2: Plan generation by STRIPS for moving from initial to goal state in Figure 3.4

1:	2:	3:	4:
On(B,A)	Clear(A)	Holding(B)	PickUp(B)
OnTable(A)	Holding(B)	Stack(B,A)	Stack(B,A)
	Stack(B,A)	OnTable(A)	OnTable(A)
	OnTable(A)		

However, this elementary form of means–end analysis is not sufficiently complex to deal with even some quite straightforward tasks involving multiple goal conditions. Consider the situation shown in Figure 3.5. It is quite obvious to us that the goal state can be achieved by unstacking C from A and placing it on the table, then stacking B on C and A on B. Perhaps surprisingly, no early planner could cope with this task.

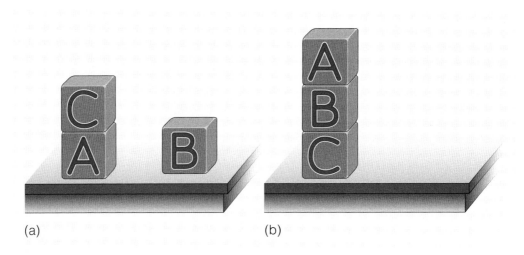

(a)   (b)

Figure 3.5   Another problem in the Blocks World. (a) shows the initial state. (b) shows the goal state

Let's express the original and goal states in the logical notation we've been using.

Initial state: *On(C,A)* ∧ *OnTable(A)* ∧ *OnTable(B)*

Goal state: *On(A,B)* ∧ *On(B,C)* ∧ *OnTable(C)*

There are three sub-plans to be solved – *On(A,B)*, *On(B,C)* and *OnTable(C)*. A planner could choose to proceed in one of two ways.

▶   The first is to complete the sub-plan of placing A on B. Since Block A is not free, Block C must first be unstacked using *UnStack(C,A)* and then *PutDown(C)* – incidentally also completing the sub-plan of placing C on the table. The blocks now resemble Figure 3.6(b).

   With Block A free, the planner is then able to complete the sub-plan of stacking A on B – it would *PickUp(A)* and *Stack(A,B)*. This sub-plan is complete and is removed from the agenda. The state now is illustrated in Figure 3.6(c).

   The planner must now try to complete the sub-problem of stacking B on C. It will determine that Block A must be unstacked from Block B and placed on the table (see Figure 3.6(d)). Block B can then be stacked on Block C (see Figure 3.6(e)). The sub-plan is completed and removed from the agenda. The planner has no further problems to solve and stops work – but the final goal state has not been achieved.

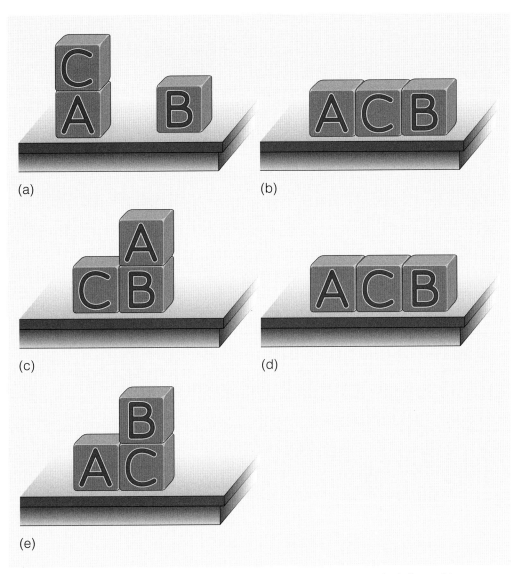

Figure 3.6   An example of a planner encountering the Sussman anomaly. It first achieves
On(A,B) (c), and then *On(B,C)* (e)

▶   A second approach would be for the planner to first attempt the sub-plan of stacking
Block B on Block C. Since Block B is free, the planner can simply *PickUp(B)* and
Stack(B,C). The sub-plan *On(B,C)* has been solved and is removed from the list
(see Figure 3.7(b)).

The next sub-plan is to stack Block A on Block B. In order to solve this, the block
must be freed, the planner performs *UnStack(B,C)* (see Figure 3.7(c)), then
UnStack(C,A) (see Figure 3.7(d)). Finally, it can *PickUp(A)* and *Stack(A,B)* to solve
the final sub-problem (see Figure 3.7(e)). With no unsolved sub-plan the planner
completes its work with the main problem still unsolved.

Figure 3.7   A second example of a planner encountering the Sussman anomaly. It first achieves *On(B,C)* (b) then achieves *On(A,B)* (e)

It is clear from these examples that each of the sub-plans in the main plan have been completed, but it is equally clear that not all of the sub-plans are complete at the end of the plan – some of the sub-plans have been undone by later actions.

So the simple means–end analysis planners of early AI foundered on what came to be termed the **Sussman anomaly** . More advanced planners not only complete the main plan by completing individual sub-plans, but also check that the end results of individual sub-plans remain valid after later operations have been completed. This led to the development of **partial-order planning systems**. These systems work in much the same way as I have described, but they do not assume that all the steps in each of the sub-plans follow directly one from the other. Instead, the planner initially only commits itself to ensuring that the operations for each sub-plan occur in order, but they can be preceded, followed or interleaved with steps from other sub-plans. Once all the actions for each sub-plan have been described, the planner then attempts to combine the actions in such a way as to minimise clobbering. If clobbering is unavoidable, the planner must create plans to repair the damage done.

The technical term for when completing one sub-plan undoes the achievement of another is **clobbering**.

2.3 Microworlds

Let's stand back for a moment and consider broader questions about planning in the STRIPS model. How well does it work? And how good a model of the planning process is it?

Exercise 3.2

Think about these questions for a moment. Is the STRIPS approach a realistic model of how we actually do planning? You might compare the model with any intuitive ideas you may have about how humans plan – and, as I suggested earlier, planning can involve anything from very simple tasks, such as stacking blocks, all the way through to organising a military campaign involving many vast armies. Can you see any drawbacks to the STRIPS approach?

Discussion ....

Quite a few questions and objections came into my mind as I pondered these questions. Is this *really* how humans make plans? It may be that we have to be as systematic as this when tackling very complex problems (although the whole paraphernalia of agenda, sub-plans, partial order systems, Sussmann anomalies, and so on, seem pretty alien). But what about apparently easy problems like stacking blocks? Do we *really* plan in this algorithmic way, even unconsciously? To me, it seems rather improbable.

A second disquiet I felt was about the whole idea of the Blocks World itself. STRIPS planning seems quite cumbersome, even for a world of a few uniform blocks, but we all know the real world is not remotely as simple as that. How well does the STRIPS model scale up to real problems?

Blocks World is the classic example of what AI researchers call a **microworld**. Microworlds have played a crucial role in the development of Symbolic AI systems. Generating a general-purpose intelligent machine might be the ultimate aim of AI, but researchers accepted from the start that this could never be achieved at a single attempt. You may remember from Block 1 that McCarthy's original proposal for the Dartmouth Summer Conference recognised this – he suggested that research had to begin with very small problems and simple systems, and build from there, with lessons being learnt at each step. Instead of attempting to develop a general-purpose intelligent machine, it was obviously sensible to start by building systems which could handle only *one* type of intelligent task. Moreover, the sheer complexity of the world is such that humans spend most of their childhoods learning to understand it. So, developing intelligent machines to work with *simplified* versions of the world also seems a very reasonable approach. As our systems become more sophisticated and better able to cope with the tasks presented to them, we can then increase the variety of the tasks and the complexity of their environment.

Unfortunately, these seemingly rational assumptions have led to problems. McCarthy's original proposal may, in the opinion of some, have become Symbolic AI's greatest curse. There have been many apparent successes in AI – systems that perform well with restricted tasks, and in their initial, limited settings. STRIPS is a good example of one. But their developers have faced problems when they have later attempted to scale up their systems to deal with more complex and varied tasks and environments. This has been partly due to the phenomenon known as the **combinatorial explosion**, which you met briefly in Block 1, and which refers to the fact that the numbers of combinations of constituents of a problem increases exponentially with the number of constituents. The Travelling Salesman Problem (TSP, described in Block 1) is the most quoted example: the number of possible tours explodes as the number of towns increases.

Another well-known problem – the knapsack problem – provides a further example of a combinatorial explosion. The task is to fill a knapsack (with a limited capacity) with a number of packages (each with a different weight and value) so that the total value of the packages is maximal. This problem has been proven to be at least as hard as every other problem: there is no known way of solving it beyond trying all possible combinations of packages. So, like all optimisation problems, it is a search problem.

Exercise 3.3

How many ways are there of selecting one or more packages from a collection of two packages? From a collection of three packages? From a collection of n packages?

Discussion ....

Given two packages to choose from, there are only $2 + 1 = 3$ combinations to try; if there are three packages, there are $3 + 3 + 1 = 7$ combinations; four packages give $4 + 6 + 4 + 1 = 15$ combinations. In general, there are $2^n - 1$ combinations to try for n packages.

You can probably see how the same problem might crop up in Blocks World. Just try adding more blocks.

This problem of promising systems not being able to scale up to real-world challenges has led to many of them being 'trapped' in microworlds, which have little resemblance or relevance to the world at large. I'll return to this issue in a little more detail in Unit 4. However, microworlds still have an important role to play in AI research for their ability to act as a 'nursery' in which new ideas can be explored.

SAQ 3.6

Briefly explain what are meant by microworlds and identify the main problems associated with them.

ANSWER..

Microworlds are simplified models of real situations. They are used when developing AI systems so that those systems need not deal with the full complexity of the real world at the start. Unfortunately, many techniques that are successful in microworlds cannot be scaled up to levels of real-world complexity.

As with all nurseries, though, we have to venture outside them sometime. Moving systems out of the laboratories and into the challenging, puzzling, confused and dangerous real world is a major challenge to AI: nowhere more so than in the field of *robotics*.

3 Robots

Moving intelligent systems out of the laboratory and into the real world has proved a great challenge, nowhere more so than in the field of robotics. But along with the inevitable failures, there have been real successes.

Let's clarify one point before I start. The only 'robots' I'm considering in this section are the devices that truly deserve the name: embodied systems that function autonomously in the world. This distinguishes them from remote-controlled machines, such as bomb disposal systems, unmanned aerial vehicles (UAVs), sometimes known as 'drones', and virtual robots, existing only in the memory of a computer. It also distinguishes true robots from the industrial manufacturing machines, most of which are relatively static devices, designed to follow pre-programmed (though complex) procedures with little, if any, variation or decision making involved. What I want to discuss in this section are the robots that interact with the world, choosing and executing their own courses of action.

I start with Shakey, a pioneering autonomous robot. While Shakey's performance was poor, its design was seminal and has influenced a whole generation of roboticists. I'll move on from there to discuss one of the highest profile applications of robotics, that of space exploration, where the story is one of unmanned probes with increasing autonomy. Finally, I'll end the section with a brief look at progress in one of the most cutting-edge research areas today, the development of autonomous vehicles.

3.1 Shakey the robot

Stanford Robotics Institute's Shakey is one of the most significant robots ever created. Between 1966 and 1972 Shakey became the first intelligent mobile system to reason about its actions. Until recently, its design has been the groundwork for that of almost all other mobile robots. Figure 3.8 over the page shows the main components of Shakey.

Exercise 3.4

View the Stanford video of Shakey, available on the course DVD. Filmed in the 1970s, you will find that, as well as being a dreadful fashion warning, it is a detailed presentation of the Stanford work.

Make a few notes on the main points. From the video, it is easy to see where Shakey got its name.

Discussion ....

Shakey stood about the height of a person and comprised a squat box of electronics mounted on small motorised wheels and topped with a slender tower. The tower contained a rangefinder and moveable television camera through which the robot could view its surroundings. Shakey was also able to sense its world directly through a front-mounted touch bar that detected if it bumped into any objects. The relatively primitive state of 1960s microelectronics precluded Shakey from doing all of its own computation onboard. Instead, sensor information was relayed from the robot to a remote minicomputer with instructions returning along the same path.

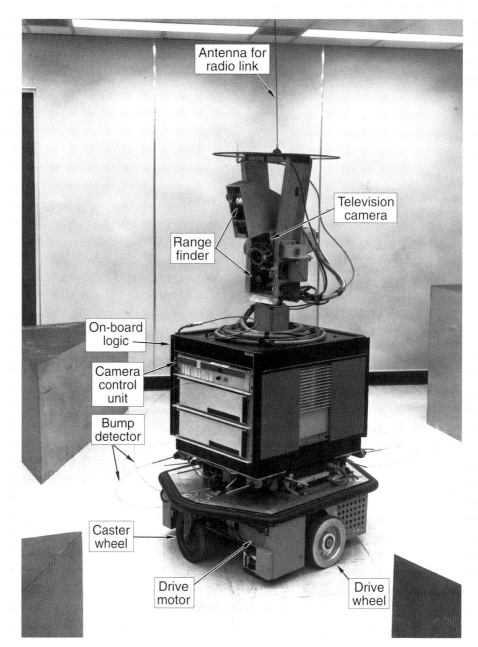

Figure 3.8   Shakey the robot

Shakey lived in an evenly lit indoor environment consisting of a set of rectangular rooms with walls and doorways. The rooms contained brightly coloured geometric blocks which the robot was expected to avoid or move. Shakey's affectionate name was a consequence of its stop–go progress, accompanied by a great deal of wobbling, when it seemed that the fragile machine would topple to the ground.

The robot could be programmed to perform simple tasks such as going from one room to another, or moving a block from one room into an adjoining room. These tasks were written in a restricted subset of English which was then interpreted into predicate logic.

The software was designed in a series of layers:

1   The lowest layer handled primitive low-level actions and directly controlled the robot's hardware. These low-level actions were accessed through the overlying layer of intermediate-level actions, each handcrafted by Shakey's designers to solve a well-defined, specific problem. The intermediate-level actions were concerned with the robot's own physical capabilities such as 'push' and 'go to'.

2   Above this was the planning layer (using STRIPS), which sought general solutions to larger problems by assembling plans of intermediate level actions. In a conventional planning system, if Shakey had developed a sub-plan to move from Room A to Room B, it would need to develop an entirely new sub-plan to move from Room B to Room C. STRIPS was capable of generalising the sub-plan of moving from Room A to Room B into a new general sub-plan that moved from Room x to Room y. The general sub-plan, known as a MACROP (MACRo OPeration), was stored for later use. So if Shakey later needed to travel from one room to another, it would take the MACROP and substitute the names of the actual rooms for the general values stored there. The new specific sub-plan would then be added to Shakey's plan.

3   Execution of the plan was handled by the final layer, called PLANEX. This exercised overall control of the robot by calling the intermediate level actions in the order laid out in the plan. PLANEX would only call an action when it was sure that the previous action had been completed successfully and that the next action was still required to complete the entire plan. It could detect if the current plan was not working towards a goal, in which case it could either ask STRIPS for a new plan, or *in extremis*, call for human intervention over a teletype terminal.

Shakey deserves to be remembered as a huge breakthrough in robotics technology, not only because of its sophisticated planning software, but also because of its ability to recognise its surroundings. Shakey did not receive all of its information about the world from its programmers. It derived much of its information about its environment directly, using the video camera. Images of the blocks were processed by an early form of vision analysis, with the minicomputer isolating the blocks from their background, identifying their shapes and applying geometric knowledge to reason about their relative positions and groupings. Even today, vision analysis is an exceptionally challenging problem for computers; in the 1960s, it seemed almost insurmountable and, in fact, much of Shakey's processing time was spent on this task. As a consequence, it was not uncommon for the robot to take days to complete a plan.

If Shakey were to be implemented using modern technology, this sluggishness might to some extent be overcome. The XDS-940 minicomputer that originally controlled the robot could store just 64 000 24-bit words in excruciatingly slow core memory. Likewise, Shakey attempted to perform vision analysis using software, where a modern robot would use much faster specialised hardware.

Today, Shakey has been retired as a permanent exhibit at the Computer History Museum in Mountain View, California.

3.2 Robots in space

You will have noted that Shakey, too, inhabited a microworld: even lighting, geometrically simple objects, and so on. But if robots are to be any use they must operate in the world outside the laboratory. In fact, we often want robots to work in parts of the world that are too difficult and dangerous for humans. And where is more difficult and dangerous than space?

In 1970, the Soviet Union's Moon probe *Lunokhod 1* became the first remotely operated vehicle to explore another world. *Lunokhod* (see Figure 3.9) resembled a tub mounted on eight wheels and weighed over three-quarters of a ton. Its purpose was to trundle across the lunar surface taking photographs, examining the composition of the lunar surface and performing observations of the Sun. The system explored the Moon for eleven months, travelling some six and a half miles over rough terrain; its successor, *Lunokhod 2*, remained active for only four months but completed more than 35 kilometres before suddenly failing.

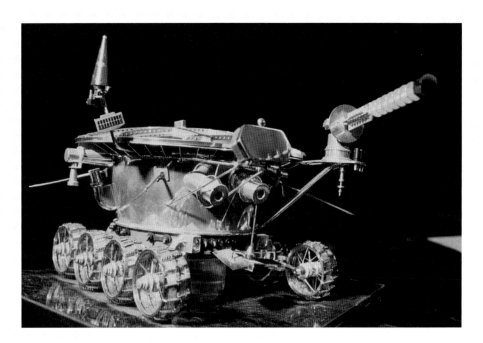

Figure 3.9   The Soviet Union's *Lunokhod* lunar rover. The front of the rover is towards the right of the photograph and the twin television cameras are the dark circular objects resembling eyes projecting from the main body of the machine. Signals from these cameras were transmitted in real time to the machine's operators back on Earth

The technology of the time was quite inadequate for the *Lunokhod* robots to be autonomous in any way: they had to be fully controlled from Earth. Human operators guided the machines using a constant television feed from the Moon, and were able to direct the robot around obstacles and over some very challenging terrain. It takes almost two seconds for a television signal to travel from the Moon to the Earth and back again, so *Lunokhod*'s drivers were trained to anticipate collisions and take timely avoiding actions.

The Soviet Union continued work on a generation of planetary rovers, known as Marsokhods, which were intended to explore the surface of Mars. But a major challenge for the designers was how to control these machines. Even when Mars and Earth are at their closest, a message takes over four minutes to travel between them. A remotely operated rover akin to *Lunokhod could* in theory be controlled from Earth, with operators inching it across the Martian surface and waiting for the results to trickle back from the probe. Primitive Marsokhods were landed on Mars in 1971 by the *Mars 2* and *Mars 3* spacecraft, but in each case the lander failed before any useful work could be done. In 1989, the *Phobos 2* spacecraft carried a hopping robot that would have explored the Martian moon Phobos, but both robot and spacecraft were lost due to a computer malfunction during the approach.

The first successful Mars rover was the ten-kilogram six-wheeled *Sojourner*, part of the 1997 NASA *Mars Pathfinder* mission (see Figure 3.10). *Sojourner* remained active for eighty-three days, far exceeding its builder's expectations, but it was still a long way from being an ideal autonomous rover. Instead of relying on its own internal navigation and collision avoidance systems, the robot used images from the lander to fix the positions of surrounding objects. On landing, the main *Pathfinder* spacecraft extended stereoscopic cameras, which surveyed the lander's immediate surroundings. The support team on Earth was then able to construct a three-dimensional map of the region around the spacecraft, based on this survey, and to plot a route for the robot that would avoid the roughest terrain and larger rocks. Once a complete route had been plotted, it was transmitted to the rover, which would then gingerly traverse it at a rate of about half an inch (12 millimetres) per minute.

Figure 3.10   A Martian panorama taken by the *MarsPathfinder* lander, parts of which can be seen at the bottom of the image. The *Sojourner* rover can be seen taking a sample of the large boulder (nicknamed Yogi) in the middle right of the photograph. To give some idea of scale, *Sojourner* is a little over 60 centimetres in length

Objects relatively close to the lander could be positioned extremely accurately, but the locations of more distant objects were far less precisely known. Beyond a certain distance there was a constant risk that the tiny *Sojourner* would encounter an obstacle that would prove fatal. As a result, the robot was confined to a region within a few hundred yards of its landing site. Whilst this might seem limiting, the system had never been intended to demonstrate new technologies. As a space exploration vehicle, it proved to be a brilliant success and encouraged future robotic exploration of the planets.

SAQ 3.7

To what extent could *Lunokhod* and *Pathfinder/Sojourner* be characterised as 'robots', as I defined the term at the start of this section?

ANSWER...

Lunokhod is not a robot in our sense, as it was completely controlled from Earth; it was not autonomous in any way. *Sojourner* had a certain amount of autonomy: it would follow the course on its own, provided this was defined for it back on Earth. However, this hardly amounts to true autonomy, as it didn't pick its own route.

Mars Pathfinder and *Sojourner* were trailblazers for NASA's second Mars rover mission, a pair of robots called the Mars Expeditionary Rovers (MERs) (see Figure 3.11). These robotic geologists were designed to search the planet for evidence of water, a vital component in the evolution of life. Each MER was intended to be a large robot that would not be tied to a base station, travelling comparatively large distances over the Martian surface, continually meeting new and unforeseen challenges.

The Mars Expeditionary Rover home page is at
http://www.jpl.nasa.gov/missions/mer/

Figure 3.11   A computer-generated image of one of the two Mars Expeditionary Rovers working on the Martian surface. The robot is facing towards the right. Navigation is controlled through two cameras mounted on top of the tall boom; hazard avoidance is controlled using two smaller cameras mounted at the front of the robot just below the flat solar panels

The MERs were designed as semi-autonomous vehicles. Major objectives would be sent from Earth, but the rovers would be capable of making minor decisions for themselves. This approach allowed experts on Earth to identify sites of interest at which the rover could deploy its scientific instruments or lay down waypoints for the next section of the journey, whilst leaving it to the rover to work out for itself how to complete those tasks. Each rover uses a pair of high-resolution television cameras to create an image of its surroundings, which is then beamed back to Earth. There, controllers create a three-dimensional map of the terrain from which they identify targets of interest, waypoints and obstacles. As with Sojourner, the operators create a plan of action for the rover which is then transmitted to Mars.

The Mars Expeditionary Rovers are controlled using the Maestro software. You can download Maestro and real data from the rovers, allowing you to control a virtual Mars rover.

http://rtfm.zrz.tu-berlin. de/mirror/mars. telascience.org

As the rovers move between the waypoints set by their operators, they examine their surroundings using a second pair of stereoscopic cameras. These images are compiled into a three-dimensional representation of the robots' surroundings. The rover generates safe paths across the map by excluding areas with excessive slopes, or ground that is too rough or too rocky. It then rolls forward for up to two metres before repeating the process. You can get an idea of the greater confidence and autonomy of the MERs by comparing the distance they have covered with that of the earlier Sojourner. In three months, *Sojourner* covered 100 metres; each of the MERs has covered greater distances in a single day.

The MERs, named *Spirit* and *Opportunity*, landed on Mars in early 2004 and were designed to last for ninety days. At the time of writing (early 2007), each had functioned for more than 1000 days with *Spirit* having travelled nearly seven kilometres and *Opportunity* nearly ten. Each has made many thousands of observations.

3.3 The Department of Defense Grand Challenge

In 2003, the United States Department of Defense (DoD) issued a challenge to robotics researchers; they were to attempt to build self-navigating robotic vehicles that could complete an unfamiliar 200-mile (320-kilometre) off-road course through the unforgiving deserts south-west of Las Vegas. The builders of the first vehicle to complete the challenge in less than ten hours would win a prize of $1 million (later raised to $2 million).

Competitors could use global positioning satellite (GPS) technology to navigate along a series of waypoints between 45 and 300 feet apart (14 and 90 metres), but also had to stay within a narrow route between those points. This ambitious challenge required robots to have capabilities far beyond any previously demonstrated. Autonomous vehicles had been demonstrated since the 1980s, but they had previously been restricted to well-prepared test tracks and quiet side roads, not the rough terrain of the American desert.

Fifteen teams took part in the 2004 challenge, but the competition ended early when all of the competitors suffered early breakdowns. Perhaps surprisingly, most of the failures were mechanical, rather than caused by software problems. The most successful entry, Team Red from Carnegie Mellon University in Pennsylvania had completed 7.4 miles (11.9 kilometres) of the challenge before having to withdraw. Rather than being seen as a setback, the Challenge was renewed, with the DoD committing itself to funding further competitions through to 2007.

Twenty-three teams took part in the 2005 challenge and five of the competitors completed the entire course (four of them within the ten-hour limit). The winner was Stanley, a converted Volkswagen Touareg from Stanford University; Stanley completed the race in 6 hours 54 minutes at an average speed of 19.1 miles (30.7 kilometres) per hour. Stanley used GPS data to fix its location on the map, whilst gyroscopic data recorded its acceleration, deceleration and rotation. Obstacles were identified using five lasers that scanned Stanley's surroundings out to a distance of some 100 feet (30 metres). More distant obstacles directly in front of the car could be detected using video cameras.

Stanley's success was in part due to its use of machine learning. Data from Stanley's sensors were converted into a 'map' consisting of 1-foot (30-centimetre) squares. Each square was given a value: 'free' (driveable), 'occupied' (an obstacle) or 'unknown'. At first, Stanley misinterpreted data, seeing obstacles where there were none, making it hesitant and prone to crashing off of the course. The initial error rate in the map was almost twelve per cent. After each trial, Stanley's human operators fed it the reactions of human drivers to the same part of the map; Stanley would then use a learning algorithm to adjust its interpretation of the map; by the time of the challenge Stanley's false positive rate was just 0.00002%, making for a very confident drive.

Stanley's lasers produced very accurate results to a range of 100 feet (30 metres). Theoretically, this would limit its top speed to just 25 miles (40 kilometres) per hour; but higher speeds were obtained by using high-resolution video images; these were interpreted and passed through the same evaluation process as the internal map. If Stanley perceived free spaces ahead it would accelerate to a maximum of 40 miles (64 kilometres) per hour; if it saw obstructions it would decelerate just enough to manoeuvre successfully around the obstacle.

SAQ 3.8

Does Stanley qualify as a robot in our sense of the term?

ANSWER...

Yes, Stanley is a robot. It is given a route to follow, but this is hardly more detailed than the route that would be given to a human driver. Stanley is left entirely to its own devices to determine how to follow this route. More importantly, Stanley identifies hazards on this route and determines its own plans for avoiding them. As it's completely autonomous, it qualifies as a robot.

This Grand Challenge was a struggle to meet, but it is by no means the end of the story. In mid-2006, the US DoD announced a new challenge for autonomous vehicles: urban driving. City streets are much more challenging than open spaces: they are cluttered with confusing objects, lines of sight are shorter, there's less space to get away with mistakes and traffic laws have to be obeyed. But the biggest hurdle is the presence of all the other drivers. The challenge will take place in a simulated urban environment and will include a number of vehicles moving simultaneously, some robotic, some driven by humans. The first run is scheduled to take place in November 2007. We wait to see what comes of it.

How did these machines work? How much did their design owe to that of their venerable ancestor, Shakey? This is too complex a question to tackle in this brief survey; but a brief answer would be that they use a certain amount of old-style planning approaches, but many more new techniques from the field of reactive robotics, which you will learn about in Block 3. I've put some follow-up material and links on the course website.

4 Learning, adaptation and heuristics

Generally, the AI systems I have discussed so far have had their knowledge built in to them from the beginning. However, this is hardly the most desirable state of affairs. For a start, one characteristic that we would surely associate with an intelligent individual, natural or artificial, is the ability to *learn* from its environment, whether this means widening the range of tasks it can perform or performing the same tasks better. If we really want to understand the nature of intelligence, we have to understand learning. Another reason for investigating learning is to make the development of intelligent systems easier: rather than equipping a system with all the knowledge it needs, we can develop a system that begins with adequate behaviour, but learns to become more competent. The ability to learn is also the ability to adapt to changing circumstances, a vital feature of any system.

Learning is a process of changing behaviour. In Symbolic AI systems, behaviour is governed by the *processes* defined for that system. Therefore, if a system is to learn, it must alter these, by either modifying existing processes or adding new ones. Many existing learning systems have the task of *classification*: the system is presented with a set of examples and learns to classify these into different categories. Recognising faces, categorising news stories and diagnosing heart arrhythmias from ECG traces are all examples. The learning can be either *supervised* (where the correct classifications are known to the learner) or *unsupervised* (where the learner has to work out the classifications for itself). Other approaches to automated learning include:

1 **speed-up learning**. In speed-up learning a system remembers situations it has been in before and the actions it took then. When it encounters a similar situation later, it decides on an action by remembering what it did last time, rather than determining it from first principles all over again;

2 **inductive programming**. A learning system is presented with the inputs and desired outputs of a program or procedure. The system has to derive the program that satisfies these constraints.

Learning is a vast subject, sprawling across psychology, biology, mathematics and computing. I'll return to some of the points above in the final unit of this block, and cover the basic ideas in much more detail in Block 3.

The one learning system we've seen so far is Stanley the driving robot. Stanley has also been one of the most successful systems we've seen. Another classic example of learning was Samuel's checkers program, written in 1954. In a few days of training, it had learnt enough to beat its creator.

SAQ 3.9

What must a Symbolic AI system be able to do in order to learn?

ANSWER...

It must be able to modify the processes it can carry out, either by changing them or by introducing new ones.

There are many ways of implementing learning systems. Two of the most significant are **artificial neural networks** and **genetic algorithms**, which are the subject of Blocks 4 and 5, respectively. However, as this block is concerned purely with Symbolic AI, in this section I will just look briefly at two purely symbolic approaches: the learning of **decision trees** and systems that use a variety of methods to *discover* new findings in mathematics and science.

4.1 Decision trees

In this example, the decision is a binary choice, X or Y (watch TV or study); it need not be, but such decision trees are slightly more complex.

A decision tree (see Figure 3.12) is a way of classifying objects or situations. In essence, it is like the game of 'Twenty questions'. The tree represents a system for classifying an object based on the values of various attributes of that object. Each leaf node of the tree represents a *class* the object could belong to; and each internal node represents a *test* to get the value of an attribute of the object. As each attribute is tested, we move down the tree until we reach a correct classification. So a decision tree is really a way of representing an *order* in which to ask questions about an object (or directly observe its attributes) in order to place it in the right class.

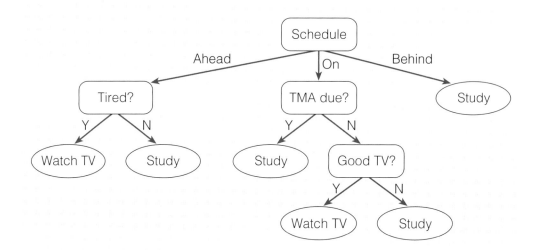

Figure 3.12   An example decision tree for determining whether to study M366 or spend the evening watching TV

Decision trees are common in Symbolic AI because there are well-understood techniques for learning (inducing) them from a set of examples. For instance, suppose that we want a computer to predict whether someone will study M366 or spend the evening watching TV. The decision-making process they use is shown in Figure 3.12. If the person can simply write this down, there is nothing to learn. However, in many situations, the decision-making process is inaccessible – like much knowledge it may be implicit. In such cases, we have to study the decision-making behaviour and use it to learn how decisions are made, automating this process if we can. To illustrate this, consider Table 3.4 which sets out an array of observations of what happened on different evenings in the life of a typical student, together with the decisions she made. From this **training data**, we can induce a decision tree that will predict whether this student will study M366 or watch the TV on any particular evening.

Table 3.4 A set of decisions made about study

Evening	TMA due?	Tired?	Good TV?	Schedule?	Action
1	No	No	No	On	Study
2	Yes	Yes	Yes	Ahead	Watch TV
3	Yes	Yes	No	Behind	Study
4	No	No	No	On	Study
5	No	Yes	No	Behind	Study
6	No	No	Yes	On	Watch TV
7	Yes	No	Yes	Behind	Study
8	Yes	No	Yes	On	Study
9	No	No	Yes	On	Watch TV
10	Yes	Yes	No	On	Study
11	No	No	Yes	Ahead	Study
12	No	No	Yes	Ahead	Study
13	Yes	Yes	No	On	Study
14	No	Yes	Yes	Behind	Study
15	No	Yes	No	On	Study
16	No	Yes	Yes	On	Watch TV
17	No	Yes	No	Ahead	Watch TV

The simplest decision tree is one with as many branches as there are items in the training data (i.e. rows in our table): each branch, each combination of answers to the four key questions, leads to a different outcome. However, this doesn't really fit with what we normally mean by 'learning', mainly because such a tree would not allow us to generalise from existing training data when a new situation occurs. A better way to learn a decision tree is to apply some intelligence to the learning process. One well-known learning procedure, **ID3**, tries to identify the most discriminating attribute for the decision and to split the data on the value of that attribute. For instance, in the data shown in Table 3.4, the most discriminating attribute seems to be 'Schedule?': if the student is behind schedule, the student will always study; if she is on schedule, she studies more often than not; otherwise she will often watch TV. The next most important attribute appears to be 'Good TV?' – if there is nothing good on the TV she will nearly always study M366. Building the tree up level by level leads to the partial tree in Figure 3.13.

The selection of the most discriminating attribute can be made in many ways, depending on the learning algorithm. Commonly, techniques from a branch of mathematics called *information theory* are applied (I used information gained in this example). You'll encounter information theory in Block 4.

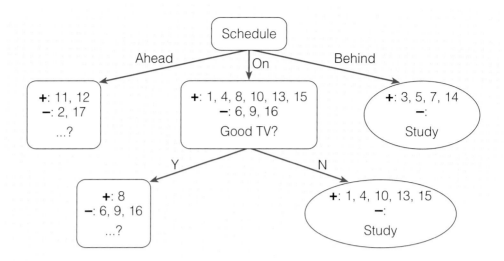

Figure 3.13   Cases in the learning tree

The process stops when we have either:

1   used the questions to select a set of examples that all have the same outcome (as in Figure 3.14); or

2   reached a position where none of the remaining attributes (if any) can distinguish between the decisions made; or

3   found a combination of questions for which there are no examples in the training set.

The first outcome is the one we ideally want to achieve: it shows that we've correctly found a chain of reasoning that represents the decision-making process. The second outcome is less desirable: it means that either there is some noise in the training data, the decision process is non-deterministic, or the attributes we are examining don't capture all the important elements that go into making the decision. The third outcome arises when an attribute has several values, of which there are only some examples in the training set. In such cases, we simply have to make an educated guess about what decision to make (such as always choosing the outcome of the majority of training elements at that point).

Figure 3.14 shows the decision tree learned from the data in Table 3.4. Compare this with the decision tree in Figure 3.12, and you will see that it is slightly different. The arrangement in Figure 3.14 suggests that, when on schedule, the quality of TV programmes is more important than looming TMA submission dates in predicting whether this student will study.

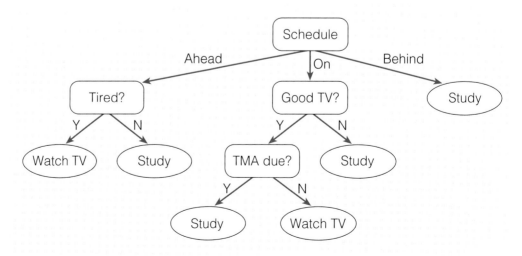

Figure 3.14   The decision tree learnt from the data in Table 3.4

Exercise 3.5

Spend a few moments thinking about why these two decision trees are different.

Discussion ....

The trees are different because the learning algorithm only looks at the examples given in the training data. By definition, it does not have access to the original decision-making process. If the training data is skewed one way or another, the final decision tree will reflect that bias. Such inaccuracy can be reduced by using a larger training set, which is less likely to be skewed. Inaccuracies can be detected by keeping back some of the example data as **test data**. Once a decision tree has been derived from the training set, it can then be applied to the testing set and the predicted and actual decisions compared. Any error in these results is a measure of the accuracy of the decision tree.

You will meet the strategy of learning from examples many more times in later blocks of M366.

4.2 Learning and heuristics

Heuristics have been applied to a form of machine learning known as **discovery**. As its name suggests, discovery simulates the scientific process of attempting to uncover new concepts or physical laws. The idea for a computerised discovery program is perhaps surprisingly controversial; there has been a long philosophical debate on whether there is any underlying logic to discovery. Some philosophers, such as Francis Bacon, believed that the rational thought processes involved in formulating scientific concepts were proof that there was a logic to discovery; others, including Karl Popper, felt that the process of discovery owed far more to chance and intuition. We will have to leave this debate to the philosophers.

Automated Mathematician

The Automated Mathematician (AM) was an early discovery program developed by Doug Lenat for his PhD thesis at Stanford. AM was programmed to explore concepts in the mathematical fields of set theory and number theory. It began with around a hundred elementary concepts in these fields, each represented by a frame (see Unit 2 of this block for information about frames). The frame for each concept contained facets, each of which could contain key information, such as a definition of the concept; an algorithm for it; other concepts related to it (either as a generalisation or a specialisation); conjectures used in the concept; and so on. When AM was initialised most of the facets in the frames were completely empty – it was AM's task to try and fill as many of them as possible.

AM would choose applicable heuristics from a store of 242 rules and apply them to existing concepts; in the process it would find new relationships between existing concepts and most crucially invent new concepts that could be added to its store.

In an attempt to prevent AM going down blind alleys, it used a number of 'interestingness' heuristics – concepts that were judged to be interesting according to these rules would be explored further, others would be discarded. More recently increased computer power has made it possible to re-implement AM in a manner that exhaustively searches concepts rather than relying on AM's interestingness heuristics. These programs have replicated AM's results (and identified a few 'new' concepts), but took far longer in the process.

Exercise 3.6

Spend the next few minutes thinking about how 'interestingness' might be defined. Write down your definition.

Discussion ....

Interesting things often happen at extremes of ranges. For instance, most numbers have many factors; those with the fewest factors are the prime numbers. If the definition of a concept has multiple parts, then dropping some of these parts could be interesting.

Goldbach's Conjecture is that any even number can be written as the sum of two prime numbers. No proof of it has ever been found.

A maximally divisible number is an integer which has more divisors than any integer smaller than itself. The sequence of maximally divisible numbers runs 1, 2, 4, 6, 12, 16, 24, 36, 48, 60, 64, 120, 144 ...

AM is credited with 'discovering' addition, multiplication, prime numbers and Goldbach's Conjecture (although it judged it to be uninteresting). Of course, mathematicians had been aware of these concepts for some time – but crucially AM had *not* been provided with an internal representation of them. AM also 'discovered' maximally divisible numbers, a concept unfamiliar to Lenat and many mathematicians, although it had originally been defined by the mathematical genius Srinivasa Ramanujan.

AM was an apparent success; even hampered by a tiny memory, the program generated as many as 200 new concepts before terminating. Lenat claimed that, of these, perhaps twenty-five were 'good' and another hundred 'acceptable' – but this has been disputed – some critics believe that AM's results were optimistically interpreted by its creator.

A limitation of AM was that, whilst it demonstrated learning through discovery, it was confined to a relatively narrow area of knowledge; it was in no sense a general learning program that could be used to learn about a different subject. There was a second limitation: although AM could generate new concepts and complete existing ones, it was incapable of generating new *heuristics* to guide its own explorations. As it uncovered new concepts, AM had to continue to use heuristics intended for the original, often distantly related, purposes. These remained valid, of course, but they were usually far too general to give much assistance with the new concepts.

Eurisko

The name is taken from the Greek *heureka* for 'discover', related to the word 'Eureka!' and also the origin of the word 'heuristic'.

Lenat attempted to address these weaknesses with a second program – Eurisko. Eurisko's object-level heuristics were concerned with the concepts under exploration, but a second set of heuristics – the meta-heuristics – were heuristics about the heuristics. They provided Eurisko with a constant supply of new heuristics which drove a constant process of discovery.

Eurisko's meta-heuristics could 'mutate' existing heuristics (including themselves) into new forms that might prove more applicable to the current topic. Heuristics were selected for use by further meta-heuristics that judged their 'interestingness'. 'Interesting' heuristics would be allocated an increased share of processing time; less interesting heuristics would receive less time and would eventually be discarded.

The meta-heuristics could even mutate themselves. Further meta-heuristics determined which concepts should be explored or discarded, and included heuristics that governed the generation of further heuristics. As well as looking for interesting concepts, some of Eurisko's heuristics were dedicated to generating new heuristics by modifying existing ones (they could even modify the heuristics that modified heuristics!). Heuristics were then scored on their usefulness, with useful ones being chosen at the expense of the less useful. These two processes were termed 'mutation' and 'selection', respectively. The idea was to provide Eurisko with a constant supply of directly applicable heuristics no matter how far it wandered from its initial task.

Exercise 3.7

Spend the next few moments thinking about whether heuristics and meta-heuristics as defined here exhaust the possibilities for generating new approaches to concept exploration.

Discussion ....

The use of meta-heuristics certainly expands the range of problems that Eurisko could address. However, as it is limited to modifications of existing approaches, it's difficult to see how Eurisko could make an entirely creative leap into a new area.

Eurisko proved to be a program capable of working in a range of fields, from microelectronics design to the study of heuristics. It was credited with discovering a previously unknown bug in the programming language LISP; but is perhaps best known for becoming world champion in the science fiction war game Trillion Credit Squadron. The game is normally played between human teams who spend up to one trillion imaginary credits 'building' a fleet of spacecraft – which then fight opposing teams. The elaborate rules run to some hundred pages; ship designers can choose from fifty options for weapons, manoeuvrability and armament, each of which can have up to ten values – and there may be a hundred ships in a team's fleet. Eurisko was programmed with the rules of the game and then allowed to generate dozens of fleets to be pitted against one another inside a game simulator with the most successful fleet being used as the seed for the next generation. Its most successful fleet was entered into the 1981 tournament. In contrast to those of the majority of entries, this comprised a large number of slow-moving, relatively poorly defended ships – to everyone's surprise, (including its creators), Eurisko won and was crowned 'Admiral of the Fleet'. The rules were changed for 1982, but Eurisko was given these amendments and that year fielded a completely different fleet of small fast ships – and won once again. In 1983, the rules were changed once again to forbid computer-generated fleets.

Eurisko's creators admit that their program did not so much find a way of building an optimal fleet, suitable for any purpose, as find a way of exploiting the rules of the game for its own ends. When the rules were changed between the two tournaments, the system had to generate a completely new set of specialised heuristics for selecting a 'good' fleet, but it continued to use the more general heuristics from the first tournament. Perhaps, what is most significant about Eurisko's war-gaming expertise is that none of the programming team had any experience of the game. All they did was encode the rules and let Eurisko develop its own approach. One general lesson from Eurisko is that discovery programs are at their most effective when they are allowed to roam through large unexplored domains that potentially contain a rich range of concepts and operations.

Eurisko even developed parasitical heuristics that were prioritised by the program even though they did not contribute to its development. One especially successful heuristic did nothing other than search through the list of interesting concepts and replace the name of the original creator concept with its own. Lenat had to develop new heuristics to restrain these parasites from strangling the entire system.

SAQ 3.10

Briefly describe the principal difference between AM and Eurisko which led to the latter being considered an improvement on the former.

ANSWER..

Eurisko included meta-heuristics, which suggested interesting modifications to make to the heuristics.

For all of its apparent successes Eurisko still failed as a general learning program. After an initial burst of creativity the rate of discovery would slow and eventually cease altogether. Lenat compared it to a small campfire that burned brightly for a short while as it consumed the small pile of wood at its heart, but could never spread to the unlimited fuel in the surrounding forest. Eurisko remained confined to a relatively small narrow area of knowledge, not linked to any larger corpus. Once the possibilities of the area had been exploited there was nowhere for the system to go.

Some of the concepts Lenat used in Eurisko have found their way into modern techniques of AI, especially in **evolutionary computation**, which you will meet in Block 5.

Bacon programs

The Bacon series of programs (named after the thirteenth-century monk-scientist Roger Bacon) were an attempt to demonstrate that scientific discovery was a logical process, and thus could be generated by standard problem-solving techniques. The Bacon programs were credited with 'rediscovering' a number of famous scientific laws, including Kepler's third law of planetary motion (the square of the time taken for a planet to orbit the Sun is proportional to the cube of the distance from the planet to the Sun). The system was given the periods of various planetary orbits and their distances from the Sun and applied a number of heuristics to that data. It had been programmed to look for very general patterns in the data, applying rules to them, such as:

▶ if the value of a term is the same in all data clusters, assume that it is constant;

▶ if the values of two terms are linearly related in all data clusters, assume that such relation is constant;

▶ if the values of one term increase as the values of another term decrease, consider their product and see whether it is constant;

▶ if the values of two terms increase together, consider their ratio and see whether it is constant.

It has been argued that Bacon is not performing scientific discovery, but is just looking for patterns in data, without putting those patterns into the context of any scientific theory that suggest their underlying causes. More generally, it has been argued that whilst Bacon manipulates swathes of numbers looking for patterns, it has no real *knowledge* of the scientific discipline that generated the original data. Whilst the patterns Bacon finds may represent real physical phenomena, these can only be interpreted by human beings skilled in the relevant field.

Exercise 3.8

How well does what you've read about learning systems in this section fit in with your own common-sense ideas about learning in humans and animals? Try to think about the kinds of things we learn over the course of our lives.

Discussion ....

A personal answer. It all seemed to me very abstract and theoretical. Certainly, over the course of my own life, I've learned a lot of abstract ideas – about scientific laws, mathematical techniques, game rules and strategies, etc. It's acquiring this kind of formal symbolic knowledge that the systems described in this section seem to be concerned with. Hardly surprising really – they are symbolic systems, and this is Symbolic AI. But I've also learned a vast array of other things: skills (I know how to swim, talk, write, sing, etc.); general ideas (the sun rises in the east, fire is hot and dangerous, cats are friendly and tigers less so); and social ideas (be polite, don't eat with your mouth open, it's rude to be late, be courteous to the Dean); and much, much more. It's not so easy to see how symbolic learning of the sort we've been discussing here could handle the acquisition of these other kinds of knowledge.

This is a very difficult and controversial issue, which I'll return to briefly in the next unit and in Block 3.

5   A note of (on) uncertainty

In our discussions so far, we have assumed that knowledge about the world and the processes in it is definite and unambiguous. But if AI systems are ever to move outside the laboratory they must face a world that is complex and, above all, *uncertain*; and they will have to cope with that uncertainty. Let's now look briefly at how uncertainty can be handled in Symbolic AI systems.

As we all know, most human judgements are *provisional*. For instance, when a weather forecaster informs us that it is going to rain tomorrow, we know that she is not really expressing definite knowledge: she is only offering a probability. I don't even know for certain that when I press the button on the kettle it will switch on, or even that when I get to work, my office will still be there – I merely hold *beliefs* that have a greater or lesser likelihood.

To accommodate this obvious fact of human life and intelligence, the AI community has developed strategies for reasoning about situations where precise information is either unavailable or unnecessary. The issue of uncertainty first came to prominence in diagnostic expert systems such as MYCIN, a program for diagnosing bacterial blood infections. Such systems have to account for imprecision in the results of tests and non-certain reasoning steps, for example:

```
IF the stain of the organism is gram-positive
       AND the morphology of the organism is coccus
       AND the growth conformation of the organism is clumps
   THEN (0.7) the identity of the organism is staphylococcus
```

Here, the 0.7 is the **certainty factor** of this conclusion given the antecedents. The certainty factors of each deduction enabled MYCIN to track how reliable it believed each conclusion to be, and to report a final, combined certainty for the reliability of its diagnosis back to the user.

Very early attempts to include uncertainty in computer reasoning used quite informal approaches. A more rigorous approach, now widely used, is based on mathematical probability theory and **Bayesian probability statistics**. In the Bayesian view of probability, the probability of a proposition's being true reflects the strength of our belief in that proposition, generally in the light of some supporting information. The numbers 1 and 0 are used to represent certain truth and certain falsehood, respectively. The **prior probability** of a proposition h (such as 'the battery is flat') is written $P(h)$. If we have some evidence e that can influence the probability of h (i.e. 'the lights are dim'), we can deduce the **posterior** or **conditional probability** of the proposition h given e, which we denote as $P(h \mid e)$.

$$P(h \mid e) = \frac{P(e \mid h)\, P(h)}{P(e)} \tag{3.1}$$

Unpicking this, we calculate the probability of our hypothesis h being true in the light of the evidence e, ($P(h \mid e)$) by multiplying the probability of e being true if h is true, ($P(e \mid h)$), by the probability of h being true when there is no evidence at all for it, $P(h)$, and divide the result by the probability of e being true on its own, $P(e)$. So Bayes's Theorem is a way of stating the probability of a hypothesis h in terms of $P(e \mid h)$, $P(h)$ and $P(e)$, which are things we are likely to know something about.

Let's take a simple example. Suppose we know that a fire alarm is sometimes unreliable, what is the probability of there being a fire if the alarm sounds? We can determine $P(fire \mid alarm)$ using Bayes's Theorem:

$$P(fire \mid alarm) = \frac{P(alarm \mid fire)\, P(fire)}{P(alarm)}$$

$$= \frac{P(alarm \mid fire)\, P(fire)}{P(alarm \mid fire)\, P(fire) + P(alarm \mid \neg fire)\, P(\neg fire)} \qquad (3.2)$$

$P(alarm \mid fire)$ is the probability that the alarm sounds, given a fire; manufacturer's tests indicate that the alarm will work successfully in 95% of fires, so $P(alarm \mid fire) = 0.95$. $P(alarm)$ is the prior probability of the alarm going off, given no other information. We can calculate this as being the probability of the alarm ringing in a fire ($P(alarm \mid fire)P(fire)$) plus the probability that something else sets it off, i.e. a false alarm. Previous experience puts this at 1%, so $P(alarm \mid \neg fire) = 0.01$. $P(fire)$ is the probability that the building really is on fire; looking at statistics for similar buildings indicates that there is only a one in 10 000 chance of this on any given day, therefore $P(fire)$ is 0.0001. It's now an easy matter to calculate $P(fire \mid alarm)$, i.e. the probability of there being a fire given that the alarm is ringing:

$$P(fire \mid alarm) = \frac{P(alarm \mid fire)\, P(fire)}{P(alarm)}$$

$$= \frac{P(alarm \mid fire)\, P(fire)}{P(alarm \mid fire)\, P(fire) + P(alarm \mid \neg fire)\, P(\neg fire)}$$

$$= \frac{0.95 \times 0.0001}{(0.95 \times 0.001) + (0.01 \times 0.9999)}$$

$$= 0.0094$$

which is slightly less than 1%. This is to be expected, as there is a false alarm about every three months ($P(alarm \mid \neg fire) = 0.01$), so the alarm spontaneously rings every hundred days on average).

One widely used application of Bayesian statistics in computing is in spam filtering. Given a corpus of spam emails, and another of ham (i.e. desired) mails, the words in each are scanned and the probabilities $P(spam \mid w_i)$ and $P(ham \mid w_i)$ estimated for each word w_i. For each new message received thereafter, a Bayesian analysis of the words it contains can be used to deduce the probability that it is either spam or ham.

Exercise 3.9

Let's say that all messages are either ham or spam, so $P(ham \mid w) + P(spam \mid w) = 1$ and $P(ham \mid w) = P(\neg spam \mid w) = 1 - P(spam \mid w)$. 70% of all emails I receive are spam. 50% of all spam messages I receive contain the word 'money', but only 10% of my ham messages contain that word. Given a message that contains the word 'money', what is the probability that it's spam?

Discussion ....

We need to find the value of $P(spam \mid contains\ 'money')$ which I'll write $P(s \mid m)$. Using Equation 3.1, we get:

$$
\begin{aligned}
P(s \mid m) &= \frac{P(m \mid s)\, P(s)}{P(m)} \\[2mm]
&= \frac{P(m \mid s)\, P(s)}{P(m \mid s)\, P(s) + P(m \mid \neg s)\, P(\neg s)} \\[2mm]
&= \frac{P(m \mid s)\, P(s)}{P(m \mid s)\, P(s) + P(m \mid h)\, P(h)} \\[2mm]
&= \frac{0.5 \times 0.7}{(0.5 \times 0.7) + (0.1 \times 0.3)} \\[2mm]
&= 0.92
\end{aligned}
$$

So there is a 92% probability that an email that contains the word 'money' is actually spam.

If we don't know anything about the domain, we have to determine the conditional probabilities of all propositions based on all possible combinations of evidence (i.e. prior knowledge). This is obviously infeasible if there are more than even a few facts that can be known. If, however, we assume that the likelihoods of many propositions are independent of much of our prior knowledge, the reasoning becomes tractable. This approach is embodied in **Bayesian networks** (also termed belief networks), which show which propositions act as prior knowledge to which others. Armed with some prior probabilities for propositions and the small number of meaningful conditional probabilities, we can efficiently reason about the likelihoods of other events.

However, the Bayesian approach only works if we can judge the prior and conditional probabilities needed. If we are uncertain about even that, we need another approach. Techniques such as Dempster–Shafer statistics can be used in these situations.

While Bayesian methods deal with situations where something is in one category or another, but we don't know which, **fuzzy logic** deals with the situation where we know all about an entity but it belongs to more than one category. If this sounds a bit odd, consider this question: am I (are you) very tall, tall, medium or short? Which category do I (do you) belong to? There's no cut-and-dried answer to this question. I'm fairly tall – taller than most of my colleagues – but a dwarf compared to the average American basketball player. However, I'm much taller than, say, the landlady of my local pub. Figure 3.15 illustrates this quandary.

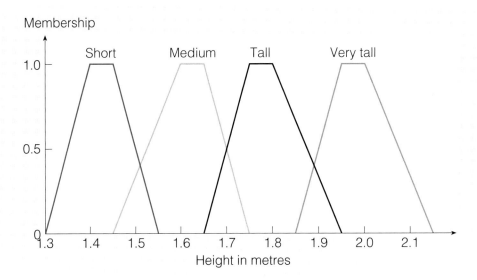

Figure 3.15 A fuzzy scale of height. Someone of height 1.4 metres is definitely 'short'. Someone of height 1.7 metres is partly 'medium' and partly 'tall'

A fuzzy scale for height may include categories for short, medium, tall and very tall. However, as you can see from Figure 3.15, the boundaries of these categories are fuzzy and overlapping. This reflects the fact that a person might be tall in some contexts but short in others. If we know a particular person is 1.67 metres high, then they are generally classed as tall, but in some contexts they may also be medium. This is reflected in the *membership functions* shown in the figure, which show that a 1.67-metre tall person is 75% tall and 25% medium. The advantage of this approach is that it frees us from having to pin down precise numerical values when we come to write inference rules, such as 'if the person is tall then ask them to get the jar from the top shelf'. Fuzzy logic has had many applications, including intelligent control mechanisms: there's probably a fuzzy logic controller in your washing machine.

Both Dempster–Shafer theory and Bayesian statistics are useful when we are faced with unreliable information. However, there is another form of uncertainty we need to cope with. We often find that we make assumptions about the world, and act as though they were definite, only to find them overturned by new information. For instance, if you are told that Tweety is a bird, you are likely to conclude that Tweety can fly. But, if you later discover that Tweety is an ostrich, you will have to revise this judgement. This form of thinking is termed **non-monotonic** reasoning, so called because the deductions we can make do not increase **monotonically** with increasing information; as we know more, earlier conclusions may have to be revoked. In non-monotonic reasoning, knowledge is separated into a set of *facts*, whose truth values are known, and a set of *assumptions*, which may be either true or false. In many cases, the assumptions are ones it is normally safe to make (e.g. birds can fly), which are believed until evidence to the contrary turns up. The key part of default reasoning is to identify the most plausible (and generally minimal) set of assumptions to assert or retract in order to end with a consistent set of facts and assumptions.

With all these approaches, the central idea is to quantify the imprecision that comes from interacting with a complex world with noisy sensors and fickle actuators. If the imprecision can be gauged and a numerical value put on it, we can reason about it and adopt strategies that will lead to robust behaviour in the face of unexpected events.

Exercise 3.10

Again, I'd like you to reflect for a moment on the how these strategies fit in with your own common-sense ideas about how we reason about uncertain situations. How realistic do you think Bayesian statistics, fuzzy logic, and so on are?

Discussion ....

I think we can all accept that most of our knowledge and reasoning are provisional. But again, this highly formal, mathematical approach does seem to me unrealistic in the context of human decision making. It rains a lot in Britain, and every day we have to decide whether to carry an umbrella or not. Clearly some rational processes must underlie the decision, but do we really, consciously or unconsciously, quantify prior probabilities and the numerical weights of evidence, and then combine these into a probability judgement?

Reasoning under uncertainty is a difficult area, very much the province of statisticians, and I have only been able to give a brief taste of it here. The course website gives links and further material for you to follow up on, if you have time.

6 Summary of Unit 3

The aim of this unit has been to consider how well Symbolic AI has succeeded in producing systems that are capable of handling real-world problems. I started with the idea of *planning* and introduced the model of this activity that has influenced the design of nearly every later planner – STRIPS. I also established the concept of a *microworld*, an idea whose origins lay in the original Dartmouth proposal and which has influenced (and maybe bedevilled) Symbolic AI ever since.

As you learned, microworlds are highly simplified environments existing only in laboratories. Naturally, then, the discussion moved on to consider whether any AI systems were capable of functioning outside these exceptionally artificial settings. A natural place to look for answers is in robotic technology. Again, I started with another early system, Shakey, whose design principles have again been enormously influential to this day. Most of the space robots and autonomous vehicles I considered in the later parts of the section owe something to the work of Shakey's builders.

The final two sections dealt briefly with *learning* and *uncertainty*. Both of these are broad and extremely active research areas, so I was only able to offer a taster of the work that is being done in them, in each case by describing actual systems as well as basic principles. In the case of learning, I looked at systems that seem to be able to derive new knowledge from their existing knowledge base, or from the world around them, by means of heuristics. Some of these system were even capable of learning new heuristics. The foundation of many systems that handle uncertainty is *Bayes's Theorem*. I looked at ways in which this could be applied to situations where knowledge is uncertain before going on to look briefly at an extremely successful modern approach: *fuzzy logic*.

Throughout the unit I've tried to encourage you to look critically at these developments. In the eyes of some critics, Symbolic AI – despite forty years of effort and billions of dollars of research money – is a project in deep crisis. Some thinkers even assert that not only is it a failure, but is an endeavour that was *bound* to fail. I'll now move on to consider their arguments.

Look back at the learning outcomes for this unit and check these against what you think you can now do. Return to any section of the unit if you need to.

Unit 4: Has Symbolic AI failed?

CONTENTS

Introduction to Unit 4

In 1950, Alan Turing wrote:

> I believe that in about fifty years' time it will be possible to programme computers, with a storage capacity of about 10^9 [distinct states], to make them play the imitation game so well that an average interrogator will not have more than 70 per cent chance of making the right identification after five minutes of questioning. ... I believe that at the end of the century the use of words and general educated opinion will have altered so much that one will be able to speak of machines thinking without expecting to be contradicted.
>
> Source: Turing (1950)

As you saw in Block 1, the entire edifice of Symbolic AI was erected on this statement of belief: that Turing machines – digital computers manipulating symbols according to rules – could be intelligent.

More than fifty years have passed since Turing declared this article of faith. Between then and now an enormous research effort has been directed towards this single aim. Perhaps, now that you have seen an outline of all this work, and grasped some of its basic principles, it is time to take stock. Was Turing right?

In Unit 3 of this block I tried to outline some of the successes of Symbolic AI – and successes there have certainly been. However, despite all the research, despite all the hope and the billions of dollars, AI, particularly Symbolic AI, is today widely seen as a failed project. As early as 1985, John Haugeland was sounding a cautionary note:

> Perhaps the idea of automatic symbol manipulation is at last the key to unlocking the mind; or perhaps the programmable computer is as shallow an analogy as the trainable pigeon ...
>
> We hate to withhold judgement ... How much more fun, more vigorous, more apparently forthright to take sides! Yet, sometimes the results are just not in. I am not really convinced that GOFAI is impossible; on the other hand I am certainly far from persuaded that it's inevitable. I am dubious: near as I can see, after thirty years, the hard questions remain open.
>
> Source: Haugeland (1985)

GOFAI, 'Good Old Fashioned AI', is a term coined by Haugeland for Symbolic AI.

Much more pessimistic was Hubert Dreyfus, writing in 1992:

> Almost half a century ago computer pioneer Alan Turing suggested that a high-speed digital computer, programmed with rules and facts, might exhibit intelligent behaviour. Thus was born the field later called artificial intelligence (AI). After fifty years of effort, however, it is now clear to all but a few diehards that this attempt to produce general intelligence has failed. ... it has turned out that, for the time being at least, the research program based on the assumption that human beings produce intelligence using facts and rules has reached a dead end, and there is no reason to think it will ever succeed.
>
> Source: Dreyfus (1992)

So are Dreyfus and Haugeland right? Has Symbolic AI been a failure? The question is a matter of animated – not to say, vicious – dispute today. But in this unit, I want to take a calmer look at the debate by considering some of the more notable 'failures' of Symbolic AI and trying to judge why they are so perceived, and why – or indeed whether – they are failures. This should at least give us a background against which to judge whether the perception of Symbolic AI as a failed project is an accurate one. My aim is not so much to offer a definitive answer to the question 'Has Symbolic AI failed?' (this would be impossible anyway), as to put various aspects of the argument to you, and to set the stage for a revised understanding of 'intelligence'. The construction of this modified definition, which I will call *natural intelligence*, will be the subject of Block 3, and the exploration of its implications will take up the remainder of the course.

What you need to study this unit

You will need the following course components, and will need to use your computer and internet connection for some of the exercises.

▶ this Block 2 text

▶ the course DVD.

LEARNING OUTCOMES FOR UNIT 4

After studying this unit you will be able to:

4.1 write a set of bullet points laying out reasons why the successes of Symbolic AI have not been fully recognised;

4.2 write a short essay explaining some of the notable failures of Symbolic AI;

4.3 write a paragraph setting out some of the limitations of the PSSH and giving reasons why it might be abandoned;

4.4 critically discuss whether Symbolic AI has, on the whole, been successful.

2 Strong and weak AI

So has Symbolic AI been a failure? Given the outstanding performance of, say, IBM's chess-playing supercomputer, Deep Blue, which has indeed fulfilled one of Turing's predictions for intelligent machines, why would anyone want to claim it has?

Exercise 4.1

Take a quick look back over some of the systems that I've discussed in this block. Try to write a few brief notes on whether you think the original aims of Turing and the other founders of Symbolic AI have, to any extent, been met. Don't spend a lot of time on this, but do try to form a view of your own.

Discussion ....

I found it very difficult to form a clear judgment. If we consider the original two criteria for intelligence that were identified in Block 1 – the Turing Test and chess – the results are mixed. No program has yet claimed the Loebner Prize, and it seems that AI systems are as far from passing the Turing Test as ever. On the other hand, computer chess does seem to have been a triumph: Turing's prediction that a computer would one day play chess at master level has been more than fulfilled. As for Turing's belief that we would one day talk about intelligent machines without apparent absurdity, I'm not sure how far we have got. I can (and even have) referred to my washing machine as 'intelligent'. But there I'm surely only using the word in a vague, metaphorical sense. All in all, I think most of us would find it difficult to look on any of the systems I've presented in this block as intelligent in any realistic sense.

I think the main problem is that many of the questions with which AI started in the early fifties were never properly debated and were simply left unresolved. The result was that the Symbolic AI project has never had clear, agreed goals. The founders of AI were, of course, thoughtful people, but they were mainly mathematicians and technologists; and in the digital computer they had a new and enormously impressive invention that they were itching to get on and use. The attitude of subsequent AI researchers has too often been the one quoted in Block 1, from Russell and Norvig, which I'll quote again here:

> We have now explained why AI is exciting, but we have not said what it *is*. We could just say, 'Well it has to do with smart programs, so let's get on and write some.'
>
> Source: Russell and Norvig (2002)

Computer researchers, then as now, are – perhaps understandably – impatient with abstract philosophical debates. So foundational questions were never tackled and have come back to bedevil the AI project. What are these questions? You met them in Block 1. They are these:

▶ *What is intelligence?* You may recall from Block 1 that I asked you to consider a definition. Every attempt falls into the trap of disagreement, abstractness, circularity and reliance on a few key examples.

► *Simulation or emulation?* What are we trying to do? Are we trying to *mimic* intelligence (simulation), or to create systems that, in some way, *are* intelligent (emulation)?

► *Strong and weak AI.* If you need to, you should look back at this important distinction, which I made in Block 1, and which follows from the simulation/emulation question above. Again, what is AI trying to do? Create systems that *do* certain recognisably intelligent things? Or create *intelligence*?

Lack of any agreement at all on these questions has made it more or less impossible to reach a sensible judgment about Symbolic AI's actual achievements. Opinion is polarised. Critics maintain that the project has come nowhere near achieving intelligence in machines. Here is Dreyfus again, putting forward the view that AI is a 'degenerating research programme':

> ... a scientific enterprise that starts out with great promise, offering a new approach that leads to impressive results in a limited domain. Almost inevitably, researchers will want to apply the approach more broadly, starting with problems that are in some way similar to the original one. As long as it succeeds, the research program expands and attracts followers. If, however, researchers start encountering unexpected but important phenomena that consistently resist the new techniques, the program will stagnate, and researchers will abandon it as soon as a progressive alternative approach becomes available.

> Source: Dreyfus (1992)

Practitioners of Symbolic AI object that their critics dismiss every concrete achievement and they constantly move the goalposts that define 'intelligence' in such a way as to exclude their efforts. In fact, the problem is that AI proponents and their critics are all too often talking about quite different things when they speak of intelligence. I came across this glaringly truthful observation on the Web recently:

> However, upon closer examination of arguments by many ... cognitive scientists ... it becomes painfully clear that both camps are stuck in an unresolvable debate over assumptions, guesses, and semantics. When philosophers cannot even agree on a definition of intelligence, it seems rather unfruitful to debate whether machines can achieve it.

> Source: Rose

Quite so. So let's not get involved in this fistfight. Instead, I can round off this block with a look at the purported failures of Symbolic AI and attempt to find a way forward.

3 Failures of Symbolic AI

I think there are three contributing factors to Symbolic AI's perception as a failure:

▶ *'Just programming'*. Some of AI's successes have not been seen as successes, but are instead regarded as 'just programming'.

▶ *Hype*. AI's realisation in some areas has often failed to live up to the (perhaps over-hyped) expectations.

▶ *Concealment*. Many AI techniques have become accepted within mainstream computing and AI systems often take the form of specialised modules within large software packages. As such, their intelligence goes unnoticed.

I will address each of these three in turn, before considering AI's genuine failures, which may arise from shortcomings in the PSSH itself.

3.1 Perceived failures

'It's just programming'

The notion of 'intelligence' has an element of mystique about it. When we see someone performing some action that we can't do, such as winning at a game or interpreting a meteorological chart, we very often attribute their performance to their great expertise or brainpower. *We* can't do it; it's a mystery to us, so the practitioner *must* be intelligent. Very often, though, when we find out more about it, or possibly achieve some of the same skills ourselves, this competence can be put down to 'having the knack', which can be easily taught (Section 7.2 of Unit 1 gives the example of expert systems needing as few as a dozen rules to exhibit expert behaviour). Once we know the knack, we often see the performance as requiring not so much intelligence, but more the simple application of quite straightforward techniques.

The same thing may be happening with actual, working AI systems. If we understand some set of behaviours well enough to implement it in a computer, there is very little mystery left. And if we realise that computers blindly follow the instructions they have been given, it becomes difficult to ascribe intelligence to them when they follow those instructions. This is known as the **AI effect**. If an AI project fails, it's a failure of AI generally. If it succeeds, the task didn't really require intelligence in the first place. To take a concrete example of this, consider IBM's public statements concerning *Deep Blue*. As you know, game playing, and chess in particular, have long been seen as exemplar problems for testing AI techniques: if we can build a machine that plays a cerebral game such as chess, we have gone some way to creating an intelligent machine. And Deep Blue certainly *was* capable of playing chess and winning against Gary Kasparov, the then world chess champion, in 1997. However, IBM did not proclaim Deep Blue to be an intelligent machine; instead, they went out of their way to point out that it was simply doing a high-ply heuristic search, succeeding by brute force rather than intelligence (IBM claims that Deep Blue's success is purely down to its ability to examine 200 000 000 board positions per second). It is ironic that a computer that successfully performs one of the classic AI tasks is now not seen as intelligent.

Chess aficionados can read an in depth analysis of the match at http://www.research.ibm.com/deepblue/.

Figure 4.1   Deep Blue, the chess-playing computer

A similar attitude can be seen with many other AI systems that are now quietly and successfully in use. Developing a knowledge base for an expert system is seen as simply very high level programming; voice recognition, such as IBM's *ViaVoice*, is dismissed as just another software application. In cases such as these, the act of implementing the system on a computer seems to indicate that there is nothing innately mysterious about the processes involved. No human judgement is needed, so intelligence can play no part.

Hype

Noam Chomsky (a prominent American linguist and AI researcher) has argued that this learning is not haphazard. He argues that the input in the first few years of life is not sufficient to allow children to learn language. He uses this poverty of stimulus to argue that people have a built-in, 'hardwired' language-learning module.

The history of AI has been littered with claims that developing computational intelligence is either impossible or really quite simple. After all, one line of argument goes, humans develop intelligence in the space of a few years after birth and do it in a rather haphazard manner of unguided experiential learning. If humans can learn how to walk, talk, play chess and all manner of other things in a few years, how hard can it be to get a machine to do the same?

It is this sort of reasoning that has led to a large number of wildly optimistic claims about the progress of AI, such as all the hype that surrounded Japan's Fifth Generation project, the CYC project, and the idea of machine translation. Here is an egregious example from 1984:

> The Japanese are planning the miracle product. It will come not from their mines, their wells, their fields, or even their seas. It comes instead from their brains. The miracle product is knowledge, and the Japanese are planning to package and sell it the way other nations package and sell energy, food, or manufactured goods. They're going to give the world the next generation – Fifth Generation – of computers, and those machines are going to be intelligent.

> The Fifth Generation will be more than a technological breakthrough. The Japanese expect these machines to change their lives – and everyone else's. Intelligent machines are not only to make Japan's society a better, richer one by the 1990s, but they're explicitly planned to be influential in other areas, such as managing energy or helping deal with the problems of an aging society. ... the new machines will:

'serve as an active prime mover in all industrial fields by helping to increase the efficiency in those areas where increasing productivity has proven difficult' ...

But these are only the areas we can already see. There's a universe of possibilities essentially unknown to us that this research will open up.

'Development in unexplored fields can contribute actively to the progress of human society,' the Japanese say. 'By promoting the study of artificial intelligence and realising intelligent robots, a better understanding of the mechanisms of life will become possible. The approaching realization of automatic interpretation and translation will serve to help people of different tongues understand each other, to reduce problems due to misunderstanding and ignorance, and to lead to further growth based on mutual understanding of cultures. With the construction of a knowledge base made possible, the knowledge which mankind has accumulated can be stored and effectively utilized, so that the development of culture as a whole can be rapidly promoted. Mankind will more easily be able to acquire insights and perceptions with the aid of computers.'

Source: Feigenbaum and McCorduck (1984)

From the smug, secure vantage point of the future, one can only blink and rub one's eyes at this. But unfortunately, we're still at it:

A search engine that knows exactly what you are looking for, that can understand the question you are asking even better than you do, and find exactly the right information for you, instantly – that was the future predicted by Google yesterday.

Speaking at a conference for Google's European partners, entitled Zeitgeist '06, on the outskirts of London last night Google chief executive Eric Schmidt and co-founder Larry Page gave an insight into perhaps the most ambitious project the Californian business is undertaking – artificial intelligence (AI).

'The ultimate search engine would understand everything in the world. It would understand everything that you asked it and give you back the exact right thing instantly,' Mr Page told an audience of the digerati representing firms from Warner Music and AOL to BSkyB and the BBC. 'You could ask "what should I ask Larry?" and it would tell you.'

Speaking after what was tabled an end of day 'fireside chat', Mr. Page said one thing that he had learned since Google launched eight years ago was that technology can change faster than expected, and that AI could be a reality within a few years.

Source: Richard Wray, *Guardian Technology*, 23 May 2006

In some cases, the claims seem to have been deliberately exaggerated, either to appeal to the media or to impress the bodies that fund research. In other cases, the predictions may have seemed quite reasonable at the time but have turned out to be overambitious.

ACTIVITY 4.1

Access Feigenbaum and McCorduck's article from the web link on the course DVD and skim over it. How much of what was proposed do you think seems reasonable but overambitious, and how much was just pure hot air? You may like to discuss your evaluation with your tutor group.

Concealment

Despite all the hot air, though, I think it's important to reassert that there have been numerous successful Symbolic AI systems. One reason why these have escaped notice is that in the modern era few standalone, purely AI systems have been constructed. Rather, AI modules lurk inside larger systems, adding knowledge and reasoning capacity. Many modern applications, which one might at first sight want to class as databases, user interfaces, e-commerce and decision support systems, etc. have Symbolic AI technologies built into them. Here a few examples:

▶ spoken language interfaces to telephone ordering systems;

▶ software to monitor and validate financial transactions;

▶ predictive systems that forecast earthquakes or financial trends;

▶ embedded modules controlling electromechanical systems;

▶ semantic Web and other search applications;

▶ scheduling software, to plan logistic operations.

Far from proclaiming their intelligence and their AI credentials, such systems generally reside modestly and unnoticed inside broader application packages.

I think we should all be clear about one thing, though. All these systems are what Searle would have called *weak AI*. A clear feature of the AI debate has always been to meet AI successes with criticism that boils down to an assertion that the designers have produced something quite ingenious, but not meeting strong AI criteria. It's clever, but it's not intelligent the way we are. In other words, having moved into the mainstream of computing, AI is now 'just programming'.

3.2   Actual failures

There have also been a number of cases where AI systems have, without question, failed to deliver on high expectations.

Robotics and the microworld ghetto

One notable area is robotics. Despite the images in popular media, and the strenuous efforts of a number of researchers, the truth is that autonomous robots have not moved out of very controlled environments. As you learned in Section 3.1 of Unit 3 of this block, the first significant attempt at an autonomous robot was Stanford Research Institute's Shakey, developed in the early 1970s. If you need to, look back quickly at that section.

For a brief description of the principles of STRIPS, see Section 2 in Unit 3 of this block.

You'll recall that Shakey operated in a specially built suite of rooms at Stanford that contained a number of large coloured blocks. The robot was given goals by the researchers, such as going to a specific room or moving a particular block to a certain place. It devised its own plans of action, using a planner based on STRIPS, to achieve these goals; and it put them into practice by navigating around the rooms and shifting blocks as dictated by the plan. Shakey's information processing was organised into layers. The lowest layers dealt with tasks like monitoring distance travelled and detecting edges in its camera images. Intermediate layers performed tasks like synthesising a model of the world from the camera picture. The highest level dealt with goals, plans and maintaining a full model of what Shakey knew about the world around it.

However, there turned out to be three fundamental, closely related problems that plagued Shakey and other robots developed in the same way, and by extension many other AI systems. These are:

▶ the frame problem

▶ speed

▶ the microworld ghetto.

Let's briefly look at each of these now.

The **frame problem** is most serious of these, and the source of the other two. Shakey's software incorporated a symbolic representation (a model) of the world around it, and this model was updated each time an event occurred. Whenever the robot needed to decide on a new action, it interrogated its model to determine what actions were possible and which of these was the best. Briefly, the frame problem is one of determining what parts of the model remain unchanged after an event, and which parts need to be re-examined. To come to grips with the idea properly, try this exercise.

ACTIVITY 4.2

Read through the first page or so of the paper 'Cognitive wheels: the frame problem of AI' by Dan Dennett (see the course DVD for details). Make a few notes on what the frame problem is, as explained by Dennett. You might wish to read the whole paper, which is viewable online. Although it is fairly long and not altogether an easy read, it is a masterpiece of wit and invention.

Discussion ....

Robots like Shakey (or R2D1), pursuing particular goals, move around the world and perform actions that change the world. But the world is a complicated place – even quite simple actions will change it in countless ways. Worse, any given action will *not* change it in innumerable other ways. The consequences of an action cannot ever be known to be limited, so everything that was known before the action needs to be reassessed after it. The frame problem for robots with internal symbolic world models consists in working out *all* the possible changes that may be side effects of an action it is contemplating (and all the things that will remain the same) and then deciding on which of the changes (or non-changes) are likely to be of importance and which will be innocuous. The point of Dennett's little fable is that this is such an immensely complex and time-consuming task that it overwhelms the computing power of any conceivable robot.

But intelligent creatures like dogs or humans seem to have no difficulty at all with this. Unlike us, to put it in entirely non-technical terms, systems such as Shakey and R2D1 'ain't got no common sense'.

The Stanford researchers tackled the problem by declaring *frame axioms*, which explicitly stated that most facts remained true after time (reasoning with them is an instance of non-monotonic reasoning: see Section 5 of Unit 3). In later systems, some of the worst effects of the frame problem have been alleviated by explicit relevance reasoning, which allows them to determine quickly whether one fact is relevant in determining another. Even with fixes like these, though, the frame problem is still a major concern in Symbolic AI systems.

A second problem for Shakey was *speed*. It simply thought too much. It could take minutes to decide on an action, hours to cross a room, and days to complete a task. This is obviously not adequate performance and it certainly doesn't seem to reveal any intelligence, since animals and humans can generally perform simple actions like these fluently and with ease. Some of the speed problems could be addressed by simply adding more processing power, allowing Shakey to make the same decisions more quickly. But this is hardly a satisfactory fix: the problem lay in the symbolic representational system used by the Stanford researchers, and was – as you can probably see – intimately related to the frame problem. Every sensor input had to be reasoned about at low, intermediate and high levels to determine its significance, even though few inputs were significant and many could be safely disregarded or dealt with in a stereotypical and unthinking manner. Reasoning with ever more complex frame axioms further slowed down performance.

You may remember from Block 1 that this idea goes right back to the dawn of AI and featured in the original Dartmouth proposal.

The limitation of Shakey is shared by countless other AI systems, not just robotic ones, and has become known as the **microworld ghetto**. As you learned in Unit 3, the typical approach to developing AI systems has been to start with a highly simplified version of the task, with the aim of adding complexity later, as the system matures. Shakey's environment was purpose built for it, with nearly empty rooms, all painted a highly uniform, neutral shade (so the blocks could be seen easily), clearly marked boundaries on walls and floors (so that Shakey could always pin down where it was) and brightly coloured, simple, smooth blocks that stood out clearly against the plain background. In other words, it was a **microworld**, an impossibly simplified version of the real thing, with all the troublesome chaos, confusion, unpredictability and anarchy of the real world removed. Using microworlds makes initial problems tractable, but all too often symbolic systems cannot cope when moved into the immeasurably more complex environment of real-world problems. In the jargon, conventional systems based on representation and search simply will not *scale up*. To this day, Symbolic AI systems can offer good performance in very limited settings, but this performance degrades rapidly as soon as the setting becomes more complex. In a realistic, noisy environment, objects are difficult to spot in a cluttered room, and signals hard to decipher. As you've seen, such AI systems tend to have no common sense or default reasoning that would allow them to deduce things that are not explicitly part of their symbolic model (such as knowing that overfilling a coffee cup will cause other things on the worktop to get wet). Neither may they have any meta-knowledge, so the system cannot know when it is stepping outside its domain of expertise.

SAQ 4.1

How do you think the frame problem, speed and the microworld ghetto are related to one another?

ANSWER ....

All the problems of Shakey and other symbolically programmed robots stem from the frame problem. To cope with it, researchers have adopted two main strategies, either singly or in combination. Firstly, they add more and more to the internal representation in the form of extra axioms, default logic, special relevance-based reasoning systems, and so on. The effect is, inevitably, to slow down performance, as the processor simply has more and more work to do. Secondly, they guard against the worst dangers of the frame problem by simplifying the environment, so that the number of effects an action may have is very limited. But then this just condemns the system to the microworld ghetto.

That many AI systems are trapped in microworlds has been recognised in the Symbolic AI community. Tournaments such as RoboCup (robot football) have forced robots out of the lab, and most robot challenges are now based more realistically on the real world. One example of this was the Department of Defense Grand Challenge, held in 2005, which you read about in Unit 3 of this block (in Section 3.3). The US military is a major funder of this sort of project, but there are civilian applications too. Purely software-based agents are also gaining access to a large and complex information space through the internet.

Pattern recognition

Some of the problems raised by Shakey's disappointing performance point to an important related aspect of intelligent behaviour: the ability to recognise patterns. When I'm in a room, carrying out some task or other, I don't consciously analyse the sense data I'm receiving and laboriously identify the objects in the room around me. At a glance, I can take in the whole scene, the objects in it and their relationships to one another. Take the rather shameful example in Figure 4.2, a small corner of the author's desk. Without any trouble, without even being aware of it, we extract all the relevant information from the scene: the objects that occupy it – the books, wires and computers; the relationships between them, which is on top of the other, which objects are behind other objects and are masked. Interpreting the printed characters on the books is part of the same process: the titles spring out at us as a whole, immediately. We perform this stupendously complex piece of processing effortlessly and seemingly instantaneously. In AI, this is known as **pattern recognition**.

Figure 4.2　The chaos of the author's desk

It is not just that pattern recognition capabilities like these would be important to robots like Shakey. Patterns are *everywhere* in our mental lives. They haunt almost every problem that Symbolic AI has tried to solve. To take three examples at random:

▶ *Expert systems.* Many experts would argue that when they make a diagnosis, identify something or choose a certain course of action they are *not* following a set of rules. They are perceiving some *pattern* of clues which their experience tells them is significant.

▶ *Natural language.* When I speak or write English, I don't form elaborate conscious plans as to how to arrange the phonemes of the words I'm using. Instead, complete phrases and sentences come into my mind unbidden as whole patterns.

▶ *Chess.* Expert chess players do not seem to be brute force searchers like Deep Blue. Indeed, the grandmaster Alexander Kotov (1976) has argued that the best chess players examine many *fewer* moves than novices. How is this? Because they take in entire arrangements of pieces at one glance, recognising instantaneously which positions will be advantageous to them, and rejecting, without even being aware of it, moves that will lead them into poor positions.

Many psychologists and cognitive scientists now argue that pattern recognition is the foundation stone of intelligence.

So how would Symbolic AI have to handle pattern recognition? Obviously, to fall back on the example of my desk in Figure 4.2, the task of an AI program analysing the raw data of the scene obtained from, say, a video camera would somehow have to extract the significant features in it and build them into some sort of symbolic representation of the objects in it and their relationships to one another, perhaps in some form like this:

On(*desk*, (*book1*, *M150a*))

On(*book1*, (*book2*, *M150b*))

Right(*book1*, *keyboard*)

and so on. To give you a measure of how extraordinarily difficult a task this is, think about this question for a minute. It's a very difficult one, so don't waste too much time on it.

SAQ 4.2

How might a computer system attached to a video camera start to extract features from the image in Figure 4.2? What *are* the significant features? What would have to be ignored? What clues indicate the positions of objects with respect to one another? Remember that the computer has only the raw data to work with, an enormous set of pixel data.

ANSWER ....

This really is an extraordinarily hard problem. What follows is only a faint outline of a possible answer. We generally seem to identify and separate the objects in a scene by finding their *edges*. But how to distinguish an edge from a simple line? Probably we rely on subtle clues from light and shade for this. This depends in turn on the direction of the light, which also creates distractions and noise, such as reflections off shiny surfaces and shadows obscuring important clues. We seem to judge the positions of objects in relation to one another by again using clues from light, shadow and texture, but also by importing a lot of common-sense knowledge about the way the world behaves, such as the recognition that if an object seems to be above a surface it must be supported by something. As for our identification of the objects in the picture (how is it that I immediately recognise a certain cuboid object as a book?), that also involves a whole world of knowledge: about books, desks, wires, rubbish, and so on.

Now try to imagine an algorithm that is capable of doing anything like this. Pattern recognition has been a central preoccupation of Symbolic AI for decades, and there have been few successes. Any further discussion of the matter is beyond the scope of what I can do here, but I think it is fair to say that this is an area in which symbolic approaches have fared especially poorly.

Learning

You've already been introduced to a few concepts of machine learning in Unit 3 of this block. I am going to have an awful lot more to tell you about it in later blocks too, so again I do not want to say too much at this point. It goes without saying that learning is also at the heart of intelligence. We would write off any human or animal that failed to learn from experience as pretty dumb, and a creature that was incapable of it would probably not be viable at all. So learning should be at the heart of AI. However, although there are many groups active in the field around the world, who claim many successes, I think it is true to say that machine learning has never enjoyed quite as much prestige, interest and funding as other areas of AI. Why this should be is a question I'll have to leave aside. Here, I just want to give an idea of the goals of machine learning.

SAQ 4.3

Why do you think machine learning is important? What advantages might a learning machine have?

ANSWER ....

I could think of several reasons and advantages:

▶ The amount of knowledge needed might be too much to be encoded directly into a symbolic model.

▶ Some tasks can only be defined by example.

▶ The environment in which the system operates (think of a robot, say) may change over time.

▶ A system may discover new rules and relationships in its environment, previously unknown to the designers (think of data mining).

▶ New knowledge is always being discovered.

You probably thought of many others.

Machine learning systems can be divided into two rough, and often overlapping, categories:

▶ Systems that have existing, pre-programmed knowledge, which they amend and add to.

▶ Systems that start with no knowledge and build up from scratch on the basis of experience.

Now, focusing on *symbolic* systems only, think about this question for a moment.

SAQ 4.4

What will happen inside a symbolic system as it learns?

ANSWER ....

This is not a trick question of any kind. Internally, a Symbolic AI system will possess a representation on which it depends, expressed in symbolic form. This may be a representation of facts, rules, its environment, whatever. Clearly, then, learning consists in either:

▶ building new symbolic expressions;

▶ amending existing symbolic expressions;

▶ removing existing symbolic expressions.

As new experience is acquired, the system's internal representation will change to reflect its new knowledge.

Symbolic AI has developed numerous techniques to handle this basic requirement, among them:

▶ inductive logic programming;

▶ rule acquisition;

▶ adaptive control theory;

and many other ad hoc strategies. Again, time and space forbid me to go into any detail here: each of these is a whole field in its own right. But, given its huge importance in the whole question of intelligence, the opinion of the majority of the course team is that machine learning systems have not figured among Symbolic AI's greatest successes.

There has been a considerable revival in machine learning work in the last decade or so. But, in truth, this is partly due to an increasing recognition among researchers in AI that the symbolic model, the PSSH, may itself be deeply flawed. This is the starting point of Block 3, but my last short section serves as a prelude.

4 Coda – rejecting symbols

Over the past twenty years, many thinkers have been calling for a reassessment of the fundamental assumptions of AI. Roboticists such as MIT's Rodney Brooks, philosophers such as Hubert Dreyfus and John Searle, cognitive psychologists such as Dave Rumelhart, Paul Smolensky and Jay McClelland and computer scientists such as Douglas Hofstadter have increasingly questioned the physical symbol system hypothesis (outlined in Unit 1 of this block and alluded to in Block 1) – Turing, Newell and Simon's original insight that symbols and symbol manipulation were the key to intelligence. Although the debate continues to this day, there is now a general recognition that the place of symbolic manipulation at the centre stage of AI needs to be reconsidered.

Much of this criticism recalls the earlier work of the cyberneticists. The critics' arguments are based on ideas that should be quite familiar to you from Block 1. At a very high level, and for certain kinds of problem, human thinking does seem to be based on logic, mathematics or even search – clear examples of symbol manipulation systems. But non-human creatures, even very simple ones such as insects, critics point out, are perfectly capable of surviving and flourishing in the real world. Their flexibility and ingenuity in some areas far outweighs that of any AI program, yet it seems hardly likely that they could have the computational apparatus required for a physical symbol system, however elementary.

By comparing the capabilities of both natural organisms and our own machines, we are forced to question our ideas of what constitutes 'intelligence'. We could consider the epitome of intelligence to be the sort of abstract, formal reasoning done by academics and other strategic thinkers; but the machines we have built on these abstract formal principles have generally failed spectacularly to demonstrate even the most rudimentary ability to operate outside the lab, or outside the very narrow domains they are programmed to operate in. On the other hand, if we open our minds to the idea that 'intelligence' is related to the ability to solve complex problems in the real world, with all its confusion and irregularity, then we may have to recognise the intelligence of organisms such as chimps, bats, dogs, or even ants and bees, as well as our own. If we accept this broader and more inclusive notion of intelligence, then we may have to acknowledge that the PSSH does not hold.

This argument is expounded in detail in Block 3.

A related argument can be made by considering the computational apparatus actually found in humans and animals. It is natural that silicon computers should be symbol manipulation systems: as you've learned, that is how they are designed, to deal with numbers, binary digits or the states of switches, all of which are symbols in some sense. However, as the cyberneticists realised, biological brains do *not* seem to be designed in this way. In a biological brain, the processing appears to involve electrochemical transmission between myriads of nerve cells. It becomes hard to see how and where symbols might be realised in such a system. There does remain the problem of implementing non-symbolic systems on computers, which are really just sequential symbol manipulators and nothing else. But the question of how non-symbolic architectures can be implemented on the familiar computer hardware is a technical one that we can tackle in future blocks. As for what we get when we try to implement the equivalent of a simple nervous system in a computer, that question will have to wait until Blocks 4 and 6.

This is discussed in detail in Block 4.

So the most recent trend has been towards what has been dubbed **nouvelle AI**, advocates of which reject the PSSH, at least so far as it pertains to the sorts of activities performed by most organisms, which are still far beyond the capabilities of traditionally designed robots. As you will see, the nouvelle AI approach has two main motivations. Firstly, like cybernetics, it is an attempt to understand how the non-symbolic processes in biological systems can give rise to intelligent behaviour. Secondly, since biological systems have abilities that far exceed those of our best Symbolic AI systems, so maybe, to progress, it is to the biological world that we have to turn for inspiration.

5 Summary of Unit 4

In this final unit of the block, I've dwelt on some of the shortcomings – real or imagined – of Symbolic AI. I noted that the issue is hopelessly clouded by disagreements over the meanings of terms and over the actual goals of the AI project.

I then divided the alleged failures of Symbolic AI into two classes: perceived and genuine. Many AI systems, I argued, are only perceived to be failures, for some combination of three reasons:

▶ the tendency to dismiss such systems as 'just programming';

▶ the failure to live up to ridiculously overblown claims and predictions;

▶ the fact that much AI software is concealed inside large-scale software packages.

However, I argued that there are some areas where AI systems have really failed, notably in:

▶ the microworld ghetto;

▶ pattern recognition;

▶ machine learning.

These problems led me to raise the question of whether the central importance of the PSSH should be reconsidered, and to what extent the idea of 'intelligence' on which Symbolic AI is built is an adequate one. Simple biological organisms, such as cats, birds and insects, presumably without elaborate symbol processing capabilities, flourish in the real world, into which the microworld-bound systems of Symbolic AI do not seem to be able to enter. As the cyberneticists knew, non-human animals have their own forms of intelligence too, and maybe we could learn much from studying them. So, it is into the arena of biology that we now step.

Look back at the learning outcomes for this unit and check these against what you think you can now do. Return to any section of the unit if you need to.

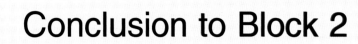

Conclusion to Block 2

Block 2 conclusion

This block has been a necessarily quick tour of the world of Symbolic AI. Our aim was to give you a clear overview some of the design principles of Symbolic AI systems, their successes and failures in practice, and the sorts of problems that they can encounter.

I started by describing the basis of Symbolic AI, the PSSH. I then followed the implications of this hypothesis into the need to have explicit representation and reasoning methods. After a discussion of various methods and tools for symbolic representation, I moved on to consider search as a general way of thinking about finding solutions to certain complex problems. I then looked at some deployed AI systems, trying to highlight some of the challenges they still face, and some of the failures of Symbolic AI.

References and further reading

Further reading

Nilsson, N.J. (1984) *Shakey the Robot*, Technical Note 323, AI Center, SRI International, 333 Ravenswood Ave., Menlo Park, CA 94025.

Nilsson, N.J. (1998) *Artificial Intelligence: A new synthesis*, San Francisco, Morgan Kaufmann.

Russell, S. and Norvig, P. (2002) *Artificial Intelligence: A modern approach (International edn)*, Englewood Cliffs, NJ, Prentice-Hall International.

References

Dennett, D.C. (1984) 'Cognitive wheels: the frame problem of AI' in Hookway, C. (ed.) *Minds, Machines and Evolution: Philosophical studies*, Cambridge, Cambridge University Press.

Dreyfus, H.L. (1992) *What Computers Still Can't Do: A critique of artificial reason*, Cambridge, MA, MIT Press.

Feigenbaum, E. and McCorduck, P. (1984) 'The Fifth Generation: Japan's computer challenge to the world', *Creative Computing*, vol. 10, no. 8, p. 103.

Haugeland, J. (1985) *Artificial Intelligence: The very idea*, Cambridge, MA, Bradford Books, MIT Press.

Kotov, A. (1976) *Think Like a Grandmaster*, London, Trafalgar Square Publishing.

Newell, A. (1980) 'Physical symbol systems', *Cognitive Science*, vol. 4, pp. 135–183.

Newell, A. and Simon, H.A. (1976), 'Computer science as empirical enquiry: symbols and search', *Communications of the ACM*, vol. 19, no. 3, pp. 113–126.

Rose, C.D. *The Great AI Debate* [online], http://charltonrose.com/school/aidebate/ (accessed 4 January 2007).

Simon. H.A. (1981) *The Sciences of the Artificial*, Cambridge, MA, MIT Press.

Turing, A.M. (1950) 'Computing machinery and intelligence', *Mind* (New Series), vol. 5, no. 236, pp. 433–460.

Acknowledgements

Grateful acknowledgement is made to the following sources for permission to reproduce material within this course text.

Figures

Figure 1.3: Photograph courtesy of Carnegie Mellon University Archives;

Figure 1.4: © Crown copyright 2004/Revised 2004;

Figure 3.8: Photograph supplied by SRI International;

Figure 3.9: Ria Novosti/Science Photo Library;

Figures 3.10 and 3.11: NASA/Science Photo Library;

Figure 4.1: Reprinted by permission. From Deep Blue, the chess-playing computer, copyright 1997 by International Business Machines Corporation.

Cover image

Image used on the cover and elsewhere: Daniel H. Janzen.

Index for Block 2